THIS NOW IS
ETERNITY

21 Ancient Meditations for Awakening to
Whom You Really Are

DANIEL MITEL

BALBOA.
PRESS

A DIVISION OF HAY HOUSE

Copyright © 2015 Daniel Mitel.

All rights reserved. No part of this book may be used or reproduced by any means, graphic, electronic, or mechanical, including photocopying, recording, taping or by any information storage retrieval system without the written permission of the publisher except in the case of brief quotations embodied in critical articles and reviews.

Balboa Press books may be ordered through booksellers or by contacting:

Balboa Press
A Division of Hay House
1663 Liberty Drive
Bloomington, IN 47403
www.balboapress.com
1 (877) 407-4847

Because of the dynamic nature of the Internet, any web addresses or links contained in this book may have changed since publication and may no longer be valid. The views expressed in this work are solely those of the author and do not necessarily reflect the views of the publisher, and the publisher hereby disclaims any responsibility for them.

The author of this book does not dispense medical advice or prescribe the use of any technique as a form of treatment for physical, emotional, or medical problems without the advice of a physician, either directly or indirectly. The intent of the author is only to offer information of a general nature to help you in your quest for emotional and spiritual well-being. In the event you use any of the information in this book for yourself, which is your constitutional right, the author and the publisher assume no responsibility for your actions.

Any people depicted in stock imagery provided by Thinkstock are models, and such images are being used for illustrative purposes only.
Certain stock imagery © Thinkstock.

Print information available on the last page.

ISBN: 978-1-5043-3019-0 (sc)
ISBN: 978-1-5043-3020-6 (e)

Balboa Press rev. date: 4/7/2015

CONTENTS

PREFACE

On a beautiful spring day of May 2013, I went into meditation in the quietness and serenity of the surroundings of the Mediterranean Sea. The waves were gently and softly touching the shore. Immersed in the bliss of the moment, my breathing had almost stopped. Shortly, I reached the breathless state.

Unlike any other meditation, memories of what had happened more than twenty years ago began to appear. They were so vivid that I was convinced I was there again.

After some time I opened my eyes. I took the laptop and started writing. The title came naturally to me: This Now is Eternity.

I wrote non-stop for a couple of hours. I have heard stories about writers that need inspiration and motivation to get into their writing "mode". That was not necessary.

It was as if a voice was guiding me. It did not take much time to write it. It was like spring water streaming out of the mountain rocks, flowing naturally towards the valley.

When I finished the book, it took me a while to reconnect back with whom I am, here and now. I meditated for a few months to re-establish a bridge between the past, the present and the future, until I felt that all I have is now, here.

And now I know: all I have is *here, now*.

If you have a chance to read this book it means that you are ready for it. If you are ready for it, this means that you are ready to live *now*.

If you are ready to live *now*, nothing else matters.

Daniel Mitel
July, 2014

PART ONE

Tenzin Rinchen

To my Higher Self, my connection with God, who gives me so much.
This entire book was written together with my Higher Self;
I could say that this book is a conversation with my Higher Self.

CHAPTER 1

The Monks

The Master is here. As usual, I am surprised by his movements. Tai Chi performed by Di Yu Ming is unique. He flows like water. We all follow him as if we are in a trance. I cannot help but wonder whether I will ever be able to flow like he does.

After an hour of Tai Chi, he gives us the signal to start meditating. My favorite spot is right on the left side of the master, where I am able to admire the beauty and the majesty of the mountains. I love this spot. I wonder how it can be possible that Toronto has no mountains, and yet, Vancouver is surrounded by so much of their beauty!

I go into meditation. The Master never leads us through the meditations. I love how he allows us to just naturally be. Whatever comes to you is a gift.

Beautiful...

After a few minutes, my breathing slows down to the point that it has almost disappeared.

I become enormous; I feel like I have expanded all over.

Suddenly I feel the coldness of the air. How can I possibly feel so cold during this time of the year in Vancouver? I inhale the freezing air. I feel snow over my face...

I realize that I am in another place. I remember. I am in Tibet and my car has broken down. I have been walking for almost two days since the engine stopped working.

I am almost convinced that I am going to die. In fact, I stop a couple of times to meditate whenever I am able to find a place that is shielded from the wind.

Actually, one place seems to be a shelter. I realize, however, that it is unlikely that anybody will pass by here, with the exception of a caravan perhaps once per month. The chance of surviving in such a place is dire....

I am not afraid of the prospect of dying. I am actually calm and relaxed. I even marvel at how resistant the human body can be, since I have been walking for over twenty-four hours continuously, without any food other than some melted snow between my frozen lips.

I fall down on my knees. I feel released. In my dizziness and having almost frozen to death, I look around at the white glittering snow, which reminds me of the innocence of a child, the purity of a lamb.

I can see a fuzzy light somewhere ahead of me, not far from where I have fallen.

* * *

Images rush quickly in front of my eyes. I cannot tell whether my eyes are open or shut, but I sense hands lifting me out of the snow, carrying me towards that light.

Have the Angels come to take me to a gate of some kind between dimensions?

"He will need a lot of *kalsang* (good fortune), in order to survive," says a calm, yet warm voice.

"Yes, Tenzin... but remember our dreaming and the signs given by great *Sangye* – Buddha. It might be happening now. *He* is back... he might be the *rinchen* -the precious- or maybe just a lost traveler around our temple," comes an answer from a similar voice.

I lose my senses... I hear a chant around me for days on end... It seems like an eternity. From time to time, drops of hot liquid are poured into my mouth. I can feel it in all my cells.

Hands. A lot of hands are touching me. I feel waves of energy flowing in and flowing out. I feel as if I am an opening to energies that are passing through me. Colors pass through my half-opened eyes; rainbows and rivers of light. Energies. River of energies enter

4

me. There a moments when I feel that I am all these rivers of light; no form; nothingness.

From time to time, I sense a presence near me. Not a human presence. A form of communication is taking place between me and that intelligent form that is watching over me.

I ask that energy what she is doing here and a clear "thought/answer" comes back: "I am *Dharmapala* -The Protector- of this place".

Whenever I talked with *Dharmapala*, I would feel a blue energy of some kind coming towards me; intuitively I would feel that whoever *Dharmapala* is, she was helping me a lot.

I ask *Dharmapala* what she really is; I say *she* and not he, because I feel *Dharmapala* has more of a feminine energy. I think she might be a Guardian Angel. She immediately sends a thought/answer back to me: "I am the Dharma Protector (*Dharmapala*) of this monastery: I am an emanation of a Buddha or a Bodhisattva. I help the monks overcome inner or outer obstacles that stop them from reaching spiritual realizations. I arrange so that all the necessary conditions for their practice are done well and without issues".

The dialogue with *Dharmapala* continues for a while. I can also feel that some humans are witnessing our conversations. I feel as if I am in a dream. The days and nights pass without count...

* * *

A warm hand gently touched my face.

"I am *Tenzin Dhargey*. Welcome back to the world. I was directed to help and assist you."

"I thought I was not in this world anymore...," I replied.

"You are in the world...," said Tenzin.

"Well, then... I am Daniel. Happy to be back...," I introduced myself.

"Daniel...we asked for permission and guidance from higher levels of consciousness and we are going to call you *Tenzin Rinchen*. We hope you do not mind," said Tenzin with a warm smile.

"There are a lot of *Tenzins* here," I remarked.

I heard a laugh from the corner of the room. "Yes, indeed. Our Kundun's personal name, His Holiness the Fourteenth Dalai Lama, is also *Tenzin Gyaltso* and it was given to him by his religious tutor. '*Gyaltso*' in Tibetan means Ocean of Enlightened Qualities. I am *Karma Dorje*".

"Nice...so what does Rinchen mean, please?" I asked.

"*Rinchen* means The Precious, The Gem, The One of Great Value," Tenzin replied.

"I am not sure how precious I am...," I said with half a voice.

"Well, that remains to be seen; it is not in your earthly power to decide that...dear Tenzin Rinchen," Karma Dorje replied. "Now you are asleep. You have always been asleep. When you awaken, you might think differently..."

"Do you mean I am still dreaming?" I asked surprised.

"We are all dreaming. Night and day. Continuously. Unfortunately there are only a few people in this world who are awake, dear Rinchen," said Karma Dorje.

"I am not sure I understand. Do you mean that now I am in a dream? You are not real? How it is possible to be in a continuous dream? What do you mean by that?" I asked.

"Have some tea now, Tenzin Rinchen. Relax your mind. It is too much for you at the moment," said Karma as he handed over a small bowl of what seemed to be soup.

The taste was not good at all. I almost felt like vomiting, but surprisingly, after a few moments, once it had filled my stomach, it turned out to be pretty good, even pleasant.

I later found out that Tibetans are addicted to tea drinking. This habit has given birth to their unique way of making tea. Tibetans in the Amdo area, for example, love broad-leafed tea. However, the tea that is mostly made is butter tea.

Drinking butter tea is a regular part of Tibetan life. Before work, a Tibetan will typically have several bowlfuls of this beverage, and it is always served to guests. Nomads are said to often drink up to 40 cups of it a day. Since butter is the main ingredient, butter tea provides plenty of caloric energy and it is particularly suited to high altitudes. The butter may also help prevent chapped lips.[1]

According to the Tibetan custom, butter tea is drunk in separate sips, and after each sip the host refills the bowl to the brim. Thus, the guest never drains his bowl; instead, it is constantly topped off. If the visitor does not wish to drink, the best thing to do is to leave the tea untouched until the time comes to leave and then drain the bowl. In this way etiquette is observed and the host will not be offended.[2]

I enjoyed the rest of the tea even if the first taste was not the best. After I had drunk my tea, I instantly fell sound asleep.

*   *   *

I woke up rested and my mind immediately started to wonder what was going on.

Tenzin Dhargey came into the room. "*Tashi delek* (Hello), Rinchen. *Kayrang kusu debo yimbay* (How are you)?" he asked.

I probably looked at him as if I was dumb, because Tenzin started laughing.

"I do not understand what you are saying, Tenzin Dhargey. What language are you speaking in now? Why could I understand you yesterday?"

Tenzin approached me and touched the middle of my forehead. I suddenly felt a wave of hot energy enter my head. It felt really good and I instantly had the taste of honey in my mouth.

"*Gawn-da* (Sorry), Tenzin Rinchen. *Ha-ko song ngay*? (Do you understand now)?" he asked.

"Yes, now I do. How can this be possible?" I asked in great surprise. "I've never studied the Tibetan language.... How is this possible...?"

---

[1] Mayhew, Bradley and Kohn, Michael. (2005) Tibet. 6th edition, p. 75. ISBN 1-74059-523-8.

[2] Chapman, F. Spencer. (1940). Lhasa the Holy City, pp. 52-53. Readers Union Ltd., London

"It is a long story, Rinchen. But I will make it simple for you. When your mind goes back to your daily thoughts and to your normal way of thinking you are in the '*world of attention*'. But now that I have opened your third eye, you are *thokmay* (unobstructed). You remember who you really are: a *Chodak* (Dharma Spreader). You can understand any form of communication. Spoken or unspoken", he explained.

"*Chodak*? What is Dharma?" I asked.

"Dharma is the Energy, the Law, the Power that supports and maintains the order of the universe," said Tenzin. Figuratively, Dharma is a 'sustainer', a 'supporter'," he continued. "It is semantically similar to the Greek *ethos* – 'statute, law' or the old Persian *dar*, which means 'to hold'. In the classical Sanskrit, we call it *dharma*."

The door opened and another monk came into the room.

"What does *Dhargey* mean? Where does your name come from?" I asked Tenzin.

"*Dhargey* means progress, development, growth," he answered. "And Dorje means something indestructible. Like a diamond. I am a diamond," said Karma Dorje and he started laughing.

"*Rinchen*, *Dhargey* and *Dorje*. One of Great Value, Progress and Diamond. Sounds like a good team!" I commented laughing.

"But *Tenzin*...what does that mean?" I asked curiously.

"*Tenzin* means The Holder of the Teachings," Karma Dorje replied. "And Karma means action, a deed."

"Yes, I remember that," I whispered looking at them.

"Yes, Rinchen. You do remember that. We know....And you will remember even more....," Tenzin told me smiling.

We had some tea and talked for a while.

CHAPTER 2

Circles without Centers

W hat is wrong out there, Tenzin? Why are these people so disoriented? What is going on with them?" I asked.

"People out there are superficial, dear Rinchen. They are like circles without centers. When you are in the center of the circle you are balanced. You are *kunchen* - all knowing. But the people out there live only on the circumference of the circle. They speak and speak and speak and their words do not carry any authentic meaning, because they are not centered. Their whole consciousness consists of the outside. They are without, not within.

"Their words are without meaning. Their mind is constantly working. It never stops. Not even when they sleep. When they sleep, they dream of others; they think of others even when they sleep!

"When they are alone, they are still in their mind with hundreds of people around and they are in the middle of the crowd.

"When they talk, the words are understood, but they do not carry any meaning.

"The only time they are in the center is when they are in deep sleep, very deep sleep; when they do not dream at all. But then again, they are totally unconscious. So, basically, they are conscious only when they are on the circumference of the circle, but that means that they are rarely centered. And even when they are centered, they are not conscious. A dead-like life!

"Unfortunately life can never be known on the circumference. Life can only be known in the center, at the core, in the heart!

"And they are waiting for something to happen. Somewhere, someday; they all live in the future. Maybe somewhere in the future something will happen. Maybe.

"But remember, Rinchen, we live now. If nothing has happened in the past, then hoping for a better future is not a solution. The best moment can only happen now, in this moment. But the circumference of the circle will not do it. The periphery will not do it. People out there need to learn to go back within the center...."

"Well, I can feel that. You are right, Tenzin. So is there a way that people out there can center themselves? Are there any meditations? Any specific techniques?

"I know that they are hoping for something better and they just think about the future. I can feel it. I know that there must be something that can help them understand that all is now. Help them become *kunchen* (all knowing) again!" I said as I looked into Tenzin's eyes.

* * *

"Yes there are some meditations.... The thing is that people out there are never certain of anything, because certainty comes from being centered, doesn't it? When you do not know who you are, you are not certain about yourself, so how do you expect to be certain about others? It is just a fog, a cloud.

"If you are not aware of whom you really are, you cannot be certain of anything: neither of your love, nor your friendships. Nothing whatsoever.

"The basic concern of all religions and meditation systems out there is to help you discover your center: to teach you to be certain of yourself.

"And remember, Rinchen: the center is here. It was always here. There is no circle without center, is there? But the center has been completely forgotten.

"I will start to explain something that you already know from Chinese Tai Chi and Japanese Martial Arts: the center of the human body is behind the navel.

"Imagine a straight line going up from the base of the body, the perineum – to the crown of the head -the fontanel- and another line going from the navel perpendicularly to the straight line. The intersection of these two points is the center of human body.

The navel is the original center. Some people think that the heart or the head are the center of the human body, but that is not true. The navel, the connection between a child and her mother in the womb, is the original center.

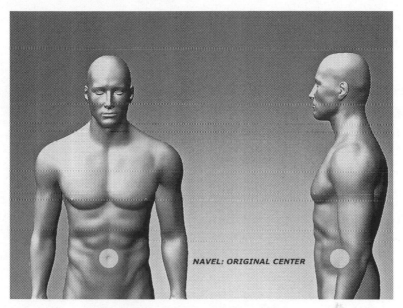

NAVEL: ORIGINAL CENTER

Figure 1: <u>Navel</u>: Original Center

"Without it, life is impossible, dear Rinchen. We are all born with this center.

"We can live without knowing it, but we cannot live without it. The point behind the navel -the human center- is the root. We need to feel it otherwise we feel empty; we are not grounded, we are without any meaning in this Universe, without any meaning on this Earth.

"The other two centers -the heart and the head- are developed later. But we are born with the navel center, the given center, the original one.

"Unfortunately the majority of people are not aware of the navel center and the heart center. They just use the head center. People become logical, just mind. If logic and reason are developed at the expense of the heart, then there is a big problem: there is no link between the center we are born with -the navel center- and the head center. If you want to go back from the head center to the navel center, you miss the bridge between them: the heart center.

"The navel center -the original human center- is in *being*. You are. Now.

"The heart center is in *feeling*.

"The head center is in *knowing*. Reasoning.

"Being center, feeling center and knowing center. Try moving from intellect to being without feeling. It is impossible.

"Where you come from, dear Tenzin Rinchen, the Western culture emphasizes only reasoning. Here in Tibet we emphasize only feeling. In Japan they emphasize the *hara*, the being center, more.

"Meditation is related with being; poetry is related with the heart and science is related with the head. But remember that both poetry and science are peripheral centers.

"The real center is in the navel.

"Sometimes, people arrive there unintentionally. That has to do with their sexual habits. During sex, because their minds move down from the head to the sexual center, for a moment, as they pass through it, they experience the bliss of the being center.

"You asked me to give you an exercise to attain this.

"There are some exercises that can help people be re-centered again. Tomorrow morning I will help you remember two of them, dear Rinchen. You know them all. You just need to remember. Now relax. Your body needs more rest." he concluded.

I fell asleep almost instantly.

*   *   *

I woke up after a night without dreams. I could hear the chanting of the monks and realized that it was very early. It was probably around four in the morning. I had noticed that the monks go to bed very early. I could not tell what time it was. My old "Atlantic" watch was mechanical and it had stopped a few weeks before.

I got out of bed and washed my face. A small bathroom was enough for the austere life of a monk. I noticed that there were no mirrors in the room or in the bathroom. I went back to the room and arranged my legs in a half-lotus posture and started meditating. I always loved to meditate. I have loved sitting in this position since I was a child, closing my eyes until I felt a sweet energy surrounding me. My mother always let me sit like this, for hours. Without special reason, she felt it was normal for me to stay like that...

Almost two hours had passed before I opened my eyes again. Tenzin Dhargey and Karma Dorje immediately came into the room. I could not understand how they knew exactly when I had come out of meditation.

"*Nga-to delek* (Good morning), dear Rinchen," Dorje greeted me with a warm voice.

"How is it that I understand you now?" I asked curiously.

"Meditation here -any form of meditation- because of the energy emanated by our temple and especially due to the influence of *Dharmapala* -The Protector- of this place, greatly helps the remembrance of past lives," Tenzin answered.

"So when I go back into the world I will not be able to understand your language?" I asked.

"I'm afraid you will not be able to..." Tenzin replied.

"However, you might be able to communicate with us and with our *Dharmapala* through deep meditation," Dorje added.

"So, we told you yesterday that we would help you remember two simple exercises to go back into your center. The first technique to get back to your original center is very simple.

"We call it '**Jungney -*the Origin*- Breathing Meditation**'.

"We -the Tibetan monks– use this technique almost in the beginning of each meditation. If we are not centered, then we cannot meditate, can we?

"So the first step is to keep a good meditation posture with a straight back and relaxed shoulders. In that position, your chin usually moves slightly, just a little bit, towards your neck; to a small degree. Part of the first step is to keep your tongue up and touching the roof of your mouth.

"The second step is to close your eyes and slightly cross them looking up towards the middle of your forehead, at the opening of your third eye.

"And the third, and last step, is to start breathing all the way down to your navel area.

"People usually breathe superficially in the chest area. Few people are able to breathe down to the navel center. And that is because it is not necessary to breathe. It happens automatically. If it were necessary to breathe, you probably would not be able to survive so many days. How would you breathe while sleeping? In this meditation, however, you are asked to be aware of your breathing. And even more than that: you are asked to bring your breathing, your *prana*, all the way down to the navel center.

"You think it is easy, but it is not. Breathing is just a vehicle. Within this vehicle there is something very important: prana or life force energy. When you do this meditation, after two or three months you will begin to feel the prana flowing in you. The easiest way to feel prana is to look up towards the third eye.

"Whenever you do that, something amazing happens: you feel how the breath carries the prana in, leaves it there and then goes back up empty; without any prana. The incoming breath is filled with prana and the outgoing breath is empty.

"When the reverse happens, you are very close to death. When your body cannot keep prana inside and, instead of being empty, the outgoing breath carries some prana with it, then you will soon die; usually nine months or sometimes six months later. It usually takes the same amount of time you were in your mother's womb where you only used prana without breathing.

"Practice this 'Jungney -*the Origin*- Breathing Meditation' and you will feel the difference.

"You will be centered and harmonized. Grounded and connected with your original center."

"The second exercise to centre yourself is called '**Tinley -the Enlightened- Meditation**'." Karma Dorje continued.

"The first step is to focus on the third eye, looking up with eyes slightly crossed, while your tongue touches the roof of the mouth - at any point of the roof.

"The second step is to see yourself as an empty vessel and breathe prana down, seeing how you, the empty vessel, are filling up from the bottom upwards, just as if you are filling up a glass of water.

"The last step is to imagine that the essence of prana is showering from the top of your head: a shower of light falling down from the top of your head over your face, your back, your hands, all over.

"When you practice this exercise, two things happen simultaneously: First, you feel centered down to the navel. This feeling is because of the second step, when you breathe down prana and feel as if you are an empty vessel filled with light.

"Secondly, the shower of light recreates you; it gives you a new birth. You feel reborn and refreshed.

"The secret is to remain focused on the third eye and your body will bring more prana than usual when you do this. That does not mean you open your third eye. Remaining focused there brings more life force energy inside of you," Karma Dorje explained.

"Now we will let you practice these two meditations and we will speak later or tomorrow morning again." Tenzin concluded the meeting.

I went back into meditation and started practicing the Jungney -the Origin- Breathing Meditation. After a few minutes, I felt a powerful energy down in my abdominal area. And I had a feeling that I am protected. I continued the meditation for almost an hour.

I then continued with the Tinley -the Enlightened- Meditation. I really enjoyed seeing myself as an empty vessel and when I breathed in, I could really feel prana coming inside me from down, upwards.

When I did the third step – which was to imagine the essence of prana showering me from the top of my head downwards, I could also feel a sweet taste in my mouth. My saliva had become very sweet, almost like honey.

*   *   *

During the next two weeks my body had recovered completely. I started to practice some physical exercises again, as well as Tai Chi.

The monks did not take too much notice of me. From time to time, both my teachers, Tenzin Dhargey and Karma Dorje, would visit me and we would talk about spiritual or non-spiritual matters. They were not aware of much of what was happening outside the area. I explained what a mobile phone is and they laughed like children. They could not believe such a communication device could exist.

My body had started to get back into very good shape. My muscles were toning again and my legs were becoming stronger and stronger.

One afternoon, Karma Dorje came to me and greeted me as usual.

"*Tashi Delek* (Hello), Rinchen. Tomorrow morning our Lama -*Tenzin Tashi*– will be here to perform a ceremony. He wants to see you. You were both Lamas in your previous lives. It rarely happens when a Tibetan Master -a Lama- chooses to be born into another body. There has to be a specific reason for this...

"It is beyond our understanding...

"Perhaps this meeting will clarify some of our questions.

"Perhaps not," concluded Karma Dorje smiling warmly, from his heart.

I have noticed that whenever the Tibetans smile or laugh, they do this with their entire body. Just like children.

As for Karma Dorje's remark, I knew that the Amdo area was, and still is, the home of many important Lama Scholars who had a major influence on both the political and the religious developments of Tibet, such as the 14th Dalai Lama and the 10th Panchen Lama.

I did not know what to say to Karma Dorje. I mumbled some words and Karma Dorje left laughing.

The next morning, Tenzin asked me to follow him.

Under the cold Tibetan morning sun, in the middle of the monastery and surrounded by a few dozens of monks, the Master was watching a dance. I sat behind the Lama, at the periphery of the circle that surrounded him.

Suddenly, he turned his head and looked directly into my eyes. I was shocked. I expected an old man with years and years of knowledge and meditation and, yet, this was just a simple child; perhaps ten or twelve years old. He smiled at me and I realized what was different in him compared to other children that I had met until then: his eyes.

They were shining as if he had two small lights inside his brain and their reflection was beaming outwards.

He gave me a big smile and turned his head back to watch the Tibetan dancers.

A few minutes later, the ceremony had ended and he stood up followed by a few monks. Both Tenzin and Dorje were there. Tenzin gestured to me to follow them.

We entered the main room of the monastery, where the young Lama took a small chair that had been made specifically for him.

"Tenzin Rinchen..., I am happy to see you, dear Rinchen. Your assistants -Tenzin and Karma- have said very good words about you.

"Do you remember something from past lives related to Tibet?" asked the Lama. His eyes were shining at me like two diamonds.

"Your Holiness," I replied. "I was found almost dead near the monastery. I am grateful for the help the monks have given me and for all they are doing for me. In my meditation I had some conversations with *Dharmapala* -The Protector- of this place. She has helped me understand something related to me.

"I like it here, but I am not sure I would like to stay here for the rest of my life, even if I have lived here in some of my past lives."

The young Master smiled at me.

"You know, dear Rinchen, in 1901, in the United States, there was an Indian Master called Swami Ram and he once said to his students: 'The whole universe is in me: the stars, the moons and the suns'. Now, if Swami Ram was right -and he was- why would we need to stay here or go anywhere? The whole Universe is within us! Regardless of where we are."

I knew he was right.

"Let us meditate now, dear Rinchen," and he closed his eyes.

I closed my eyes, too.

Suddenly, I felt a pleasant feeling in the middle of my chest. A delicate fragrance began to emanate from there. I realized that it was from the area of my heart.

I could distinctly remember the fragrance of the lotus flower. I had seen thousands of lotus flowers in the Danube Delta and once you sense that fragrance, you never forget it!

I realized that a similar fragrance was coming from the young Lama.

I really felt that *I am a lotus flower*. Instinctively I knew that the young Master had also become a lotus flower. The fragrance coming from him was more powerful.

I began to practice Jungney -*the Origin*- Breathing Meditation and soon I felt I had dissolved into the Universe. I could feel the Lama's presence far, far away, but instinctively I knew that he was doing the same thing as me. I was not sure whether he had influenced and assisted me or if he was just practicing the same meditation.

We both remained in this blissful state for over an hour. The energy was so soft and mother-like.

We opened our eyes almost at the same time.

"That was a good meditation," said the Lama and he smiled at me.

"How do you feel here in the monastery?" he asked.

"I love it. I have always wanted to meditate in silence and feel Mother Earth. I am thinking of meditating more and more; to increase it to five or six hours per session. Just meditation; nothing else. No food, no water. Nothing!" I told him very excitedly.

His eyes shone back at me.

"Dear Rinchen, remember that the middle way is the best. Do not torture your body and do not force yourself to stay in meditation. You are not in competition," he smiled at me and continued.

"There is a monk in a monastery on the other side of Amdo. He has been following my teachings for a few years. I have heard stories about him. He used to be very rich and healthy. He was really a man of this world. He indulged in everything, to the extreme.

"Then one day, Dalai Lama went to New York where this man was residing. The man had a private meeting with Dalai Lama. It was a *darsham*: a spiritual encounter. After that, the man went down to Dalai Lama's feet and cried out: 'I will leave this world Your Holiness and come to Tibet'.

"And he gave out all his wealth to others and came here. Of course, everyone around him was impressed, but he had moved from one extreme to another!

"That is the way of the mind, dear Rinchen. The mind moves from one extreme to another; this is the law of the mind. It happens every day; it is not a miracle. It is just an ordinary law.

"Before, this man had been mad about money and, now, he had moved to the other extreme: he became mad about spirituality. Like a pendulum: from one side to another.

"He completely changed his lifestyle at the monastery, but his mind remained the same.

"He told me that he had been having sexual dreams every night. And it is normal to be like that. He used to live just for sex and now he had become a celibate; he moved into isolation. He is against sex at the surface, but his attitude, his mind, his approach, is the same. Do you understand? He is now a *ḥrahmachari* -a celibate- but his mind is sex-oriented!

"He would go to the extremes at the monastery; no food for three or four days, clad in just a few clothes. He was such a nice man when I had seen him the first time; a beautiful human being.

"One year later, I could not recognize him. He was skinny, pale, ugly, bitter and upset, with troubled eyes.

"One day he came to me and asked what was wrong with him. I asked him what his favorite activity in New York for relaxation was. He told me that he used to enjoy listening to classical music, especially Vivaldi and Mozart.

"I asked him what the sound of the speakers was like and he told me that he used the best speakers in the world that balanced the sound perfectly. So I asked him what if he turned the volume of the speakers up to the maximum. How would the sound be then? He replied that it would be really awful; you would not be able to enjoy the music at all.

"So I explained to him that his life was now like that: at the maximum volume with a terrible outcome.

"He became angry that going to an extreme had made him unhappy. In New York he used to be at one extreme and now, here in Tibet, he had gone to the other.

"He said, 'Your Holiness you are right: I will never be angry again.' I replied that 'never' is another extreme. How can you be sure that you will never be angry again?

"So, my dear Rinchen, enjoy your time here. Do not go to extremes... However, do go through a meditation where no food and no light are provided... Whenever you are ready for it," and he smiled at me from his heart.

"Your Holiness, who am I really?" I asked looking into his eyes.

"You are a reflection of *Jampa* - love and kindness: Buddha Maitreya. And a reflection of *Jinpa* - generosity and compassion," the Master answered.

* * *

A few weeks later, Tenzin Dhargey told me that I was ready to go through a specific meditation: the dark room meditation.

Tenzin Dhargey explained that this meditation is a very important one. It involves staying for one week in a completely dark room, without any food; just water if needed. He said that only a few monks have been ready to go through this type of meditation. The young Lama specifically asked them to have me do this.

"Our Master told us that you are ready for it, dear Rinchen," Tenzin said to me with a big smile.

I was not afraid of this dark room meditation; only curious.

A few days later, both Tenzin Dhargey and Karma Dorje took me behind the monastery and up to the middle of a large, almost vertical wall were one could guess that a house of some sort had been built inside. I do not know how they managed to do it.

We went up to the top of the cliff. There was a set of narrow stairs leading down and right in front of the entrance of the room. But the meditation room was inside of the mountain. There were three rooms preceding the last one: the last one looked like a cave with a narrow bed, a very small bathroom and a big Tibetan pillow for meditation.

I went in and started my meditation. Indeed, there was no light at all coming in.

As the young Master Lama had said, I did not have any issues with the dark room meditation. I did not miss food at all and I rarely took a sip of water. The interesting thing was that, at some point on the second day, I was able to see or, should I say sense, everything around me without the need of light.

However, I did miss Tenzin Dhargey and Karma Dorje! I missed our discussions and their remarks about life, spirituality and my spiritual path.

There, I realized how important prana is for us. Exactly as Tenzin Dhargey had explained when he talked about Jungney -*the Origin*- Breathing Meditation and Tinley -*the Enlightened*- Meditation.

Basically, all humans can live without food. Prana is, indeed, sufficient. I remember a case about a Yogi who had been buried inside a box, ten meters deep, where he was able to stay and meditate in the lotus posture. No air at all could enter. He asked to be taken out forty years later. In fact, almost everyone who had witnessed the event had gradually passed away.

In 1920, they brought him out and he was still alive. He even lived for another ten years.

As was expected, the whole medical community of India could not explain what had happened. How is it possible to survive without food, water or air?

The Yogi's answer was very simple: *"Prana"*.

During that week, I realized that prana is, indeed, the essence of life. Nothing else is needed to keep the body alive. Just bring prana in a conscious way, inside the cells.

Another interesting thing regarded my past lives. Each day, and from time to time, I could clearly see images of myself in different situations, as if watching a movie. In those moments, I was able to understand different languages perfectly: Egyptian, Hebrew, Tibetan, Mongolian, Chinese, Inca, Mayan or Kogi.

I saw myself doing various activities that were obviously coming from another time; places that I had never seen in this life and civilizations that were long gone.

At the same time, I practiced Tai Chi each day for at least an hour. I could feel the room perfectly and practicing Tai Chi in the dark was a perfect experience. Tai Chi develops the inner breathing and it is an excellent tool that can bring you back to your original center: the navel center.

CHAPTER 3

The Third Eye

The monks helped me come out of the dark room. It happened during the evening, so that my eyes could gradually adjust to the light outside. I was not very weak, but I needed to slowly start eating and drinking tea. I had really enjoyed the dark room meditation.

Having come back out into the light was an interesting experience. My eyes had to readjust to the solar light and for a while I could see the colors around me as they flowed; rivers of colors and images draped around me, freely and gracefully.

After two days of readjustment, both Tenzin Dhargey and Karma Dorje were, as usual, present in the morning to drink a tea and chat with me.

"So, dear Rinchen, tell us. You liked the dark room meditation, didn't you?" Karma asked me with a big smile on his face.

"Actually, I did!" I answered smiling back at him.

"What was the most notable event during these seven days and nights?" Tenzin asked me curiously.

"Well, on the third or fourth day, I felt a strong pressure of energy in the middle of my forehead. Strangely, after that, I could feel what was going on, not just in the room, but also outside, in the monastery. This would happen especially between an exhalation and an inhalation. I sometimes managed to remain still for ten seconds between an exhalation and an inhalation. I did not feel the need to breathe in again," I answered.

Both monks exchanged a quick look and Tenzin said, "Indeed the main purpose of this meditation is to clean your third eye channel of any unsteady and chaotic energy. Obviously prana can keep you going for minutes or even hours between an exhalation and an inhalation. What happened to you comes from closing up all the seven openings of the head: eyes, ears, nose and mouth. When all the openings of the head are closed, your energy and consciousness, which are continuously flowing out, suddenly cease. They cannot move out.

"We condition the function of our minds with the proper function of our seven openings of the head. If all the seven holes -the seven openings of the head- are closed, then our energy and consciousness cannot move out. They remain inside and try to go out through the middle of our forehead: the third eye.

"Once you are able to close all the openings of the head, even for a few seconds, your energy and consciousness will try to go out through your third eye. The more you practice this meditation, the better the chances are of cleaning your third eye.

"Once you manage to clean this space, then you will understand that it contains everything.

"That is the reason why you could sense outside your body: your room and more than that, the monastery, the mountains, so on. With your physical eyes you can only see the material things. However, with your third eye, you can see the immaterial things: the energy, the consciousness.

"Basically, you became centered there and, when you did that, you became very intense and very alive.

"Anybody can practice this exercise. Of course, you had the perfect environment: your eyes, ears and mouth were not functioning at all. You only breathed. And when you breathed out and remained without a breath for ten or twenty seconds - living just on prana - you were able to close all the seven openings of your head.

"Anybody can do this exercise: all you need is a mask for your eyes to stay in complete darkness, with your eyes closed. You can close your ears with some ear plugs and be aware of that time when you are in between the exhalation and inhalation.

"We call this exercise the '**Thokmay -the Unobstructed-Meditation**'. So when you are unobstructed - all the seven openings of your head are closed – and you can easily clean your third eye.

"So the first step is to cover your eyes or stay in a perfectly dark room with your eyes and mouth closed and your ears closed with some ear plugs.

"Again remember to keep your tongue connected with the roof of your mouth and slightly cross your eyes looking up towards the middle of your forehead.

"The second step is to be aware, at that time of breathing when you are in between the exhalation and the inhalation. Breathe in gently and deeply at your navel center and breathe out slowly, slowly, until your body and your lungs are empty. Then stay like that for a few seconds and be aware of that time when you are in between your exhalation and the next inhalation, when your breathing stops and your nostrils stop working; when they are not bringing anything inside.

"In that quietness, your energy and consciousness will start moving out of you, through the spot in the middle of your forehead. Usually after a week of practicing this meditation daily, you will feel your "energetic sensitivity" increase.

"You will be able to sense and feel a variety of things around you that, in normal circumstances, you would not be aware of.

"It would be good to practice the Thokmay -the Unobstructed-Meditation in a quiet place where you will not be distracted and prevented from giving full attention to your breathing.

"The interesting thing is that when you become really centered in your third eye you will automatically fall into your original center: the navel center. You can be centered in any center of your body, but you have to be really centered there. Hindus study seven main dynamic centers of the body: the seven chakras. Buddhists study nine chakras and we, the Tibetans, study thirteen chakras. Any of these centers help one get back to the original center. The center is irrelevant. What is important is to be centered.

"While I was in England and in the United States, I realized that almost everyone is centered (or they think they are centered) in their sex chakra, their sex center. But I realized that even the sexual chakra is the most natural center to be attracted to. Social conditioning, however, has destroyed this possibility of moving oneself into a dynamic center. All this preaching, the sexually repressive teachings and social conditioning have moved people away from the sex center. The majority of people are not able to use the sex center properly.

"In Tibet, we use the heart center. However, many times I have seen that we sometimes use a 'mind love' that obviously moves between two polar opposites of hate and love. When we use this 'mind love', the duality is bound to be there and there will always be a suppressed anger that does not allow us to be completely in love.

"We teach ourselves not to be angry, but teaching is not enough. It must come naturally, from within. Otherwise we just pretend to love. We pretend it is not natural. Deep down there a fight is going on. Many monks come to me and ask why they sometimes have this hate inside them, this fighting mood. It is because they are not able to go beyond mind; to touch that level of no-mind where they are not in a polar opposite. The silent love comes from a 'no-mind love'.

"It is a love specifically in people that are heart centered. This type of love does not have any excitement or enthusiasm. It is a completely silent event, a completely silent experience, inside of us.

"We practice a specific meditation here that links all five main centers: the base (perineum), the navel, the heart, the third eye and the top of the head (crown) chakra.

"This is a very powerful meditation and it connects the main chakras of the human body. The base chakra energy, which is the connection with Mother Earth, connects with the navel chakra, which is the human body's main center, the original center. Then, the navel chakra connects with the heart chakra, which is pure unconditional love.

"We call it '**Ngodup** *-the Attainment-* **Meditation**'. We call it that because, after practicing for a while, you achieve this attainment, this accomplishment of linking all your five main centers and you become no-mind. When you are no-mind, you automatically fall from the head center into the heart center.

"So remember to keep the tongue gently touching the roof of the mouth and slightly cross your eyes looking up towards the middle of your forehead.

"The first step is to be aware of your five main centers (chakras): perineum, navel, heart, third eye and top of the head (crown chakra).

"The second step is to breathe in through your nostrils down to your perineum and, as you breathe-in, go up from the perineum to the top of the head, passing through all 5 centers. As you breathe-in, count each center you are passing through: when you are in the perineum chakra, say '*one*', when you are in navel chakra say '*two*', all the way up until you arrive to the top of the head, where you say '*five*'.

"You can also use colors: when you are in the perineum chakra say '*red*'. When you are in the navel chakra say '*orange*', for the heart chakra '*green*', for third eye '*indigo*' and for crown chakra '*white*'.

"The next step is to exhale from the top of the head down to perineum using the same route. Again when you go down and pass through each chakra count '*five-four-three-two-one*' or say '*white-indigo-green-orange-red*'.

"Then stay for a few seconds in the perineum between your exhalation and the next inhalation, when your breathing stops and your nostrils stop working.

"Do it five times. Repeat it as many times as you wish, but always in sets of five," Tenzin Dhargey concluded.

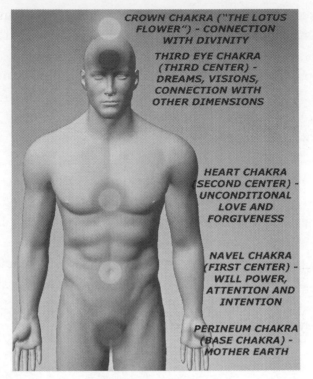

Figure 2: *Chakras*

I assume that keeping your back straight is an obligatory rule," I observed.

"The posture in this meditation is very important," Tenzin answered.

"And not just in this meditation: first you should not move from one buttock to another. You should sit still without moving or making a sound. Your spine must be straight and the weight of your body on both of the buttocks must be exactly the same. You should be balanced and feel comfortable.

"A few years ago, while I was in the United States, I noticed that few people were able to stay in a Buddha's posture: the lotus posture. That is why, when I conducted some meditations there, I recommended that the most effective body position for meditation (apart from the lotus posture) is to sit in a "King's Posture": sit upright in a straight-backed chair with your back straight and rest your hands comfortably on your lap: this keeps your sensory awareness focused inward, away from external stimuli. The "King's Posture" is a one that expresses awareness, wakefulness, strength and independence," said Tenzin and smiled at me.

*   *   *

After a few weeks of practice, I confessed to my Teachers: "I have to admit the practicality of both the Thokmay -*the Unobstructed*- Meditation and Ngodup -*the Attainment*- Meditation. Both meditations, especially the Attainment one, which reminds me of Kriya Yoga, are excellent tools to clean your chakras and they bring you closer and closer to your inner peace. Is there a direct meditation that helps to activate the third eye?" I asked.

"Yes we do have a direct meditation to open the third eye, but before telling you anything about it, you must understand something really important about the third eye," Tenzin replied.

"The third eye, being the main center within the human head where the knowledge center is, must be connected with the navel center, where we have our being center and with the heart center where we have our feeling center.

"It is practically impossible to open your third eye if your consciousness does not make this 'route': knowledge-being-feeling.

"The only way this route can be possible, is through breathing. Prana is an excellent vehicle to move consciousness from one center to another.

"Actually it is our belief that our consciousness represents an '*intelligent prana*', so to speak; a cosmic connection with the Infinite Ocean of Energy around and inside of us.

"Now let me explain the ***Third Eye Meditation*** to you.

"Again, please place the tip of your tongue on the roof of the mouth and slightly cross your eyes looking up towards the middle of your forehead.

"The first step is to understand that your consciousness is usually situated in the head center and from there you can look down inside your body, as if you are on top of our monastery, which is on top of the mountain. From up there, in that small room that is right on top of the monastery, start moving down the spiral stairs. So up there in the room is your head and you -your consciousness- moves down using the spiral stairs and stops right in front of the heart. I mean your physical heart.

"There you can see a door. Open that door and enter your heart where you will see a real universe. The Heart Universe! The Heart World! You might see stars, or pyramids, or rooms, or forests and waterfalls, anything.

"The second step is to start breathing down to your navel center and bring prana there. Do it for a couple of minutes.

"Remember to keep the tongue gently touching the roof of the mouth throughout the meditation and to slightly cross your eyes looking up towards the middle of your forehead.

"The third, and the last step, is to move your prana by breathing from your navel center to your third eye center; to your middle forehead area, towards where you are looking. This step can take more minutes; sometimes even an hour.

"During this last step, you will feel that, as you breathe, that prana opens a tunnel and a vibration begins to pulsate there.

"The more you practice this meditation, the better the chances are of cleaning your third eye tunnel and starting to see from there," said Tenzin Dhargey.

*　　*　　*

"So tell us about this beautiful Tai Chi that you practice every day. What does it do for you?" Karma Dorje asked me.

"Tai Chi is a meditation through movements," I answered. "Basically, you do a set of movements that clean your meridians and more prana comes inside of you. Each movement is related to a meridian that corresponds to an organ: the heart, the liver, the spleen, the lungs and so on. Can you tell me what you see when I practice Tai Chi?" I asked curiously.

Both Masters started laughing.

"Is the opinion of other people important to you?" Karma asked me.

"Certainly, your opinion means something. Especially regarding spiritual practice," I replied.

"In this case, we will tell you what we see and I am sure that it will help you understand Tai Chi practice better.

"We can tell you that Tai Chi attempts to create a gap. You have become too rigid, solidly fixed in your body. You think 'I am the body', which is completely wrong. Tai Chi helps you create a gap and feel that you are not the body, but something beyond the body. It is a weird phenomenon: Tai Chi helps you stop your thoughts and center yourself within. Try to understand: when you walk, you resist movement. You gently sway your body to the right and to the left, in order to balance; otherwise you fall down. So basically, you are constantly in resistance. That is why you become tired after having walked for a few minutes.

"In Tai Chi, because you move with the movements and sway together with them, you never get tired, do you?" Karma Dorje asked.

"Yes, indeed, I am never tired after Tai Chi. I feel calm, refreshed and harmonized," I replied.

"We have seen you *inside* and *outside* when you practice Tai Chi and we can tell you about an interesting phenomenon that happens in you: even after you have ended the Tai Chi practice and your body has stopped, your mind still feels it; it still does it. We have also noticed that the energy of the third eye is activated by this practice," Tenzin said.

"That is true. When I practice and then I stop, Tai Chi continues inside me for a few minutes," I confirmed.

"We can say that Tai Chi also represents a tool that prevents your consciousness from dividing into many directions. It is a tool for centering," Karma added and continued: "It is difficult to keep the consciousness undivided because our minds think non-stop. When you do Tai Chi, your mind is 'hypnotized' by the movement.

The thoughts are gone. The mind is like a beautiful blue sky and the thoughts are like white clouds, coming and going.

"Your thoughts come from the outside. Suddenly, clouds come in the beautiful blue sky. Whenever you think, you are not inside; you are outside. When you do Tai Chi, you remain with the simple consciousness; like a clear sky without clouds.

"Tai Chi has another interesting distinctive attribute: it helps you *do*. Doing is very important. The result comes about when you do. Tai Chi helps you be concerned with the technique and not with the result. If you are concerned only with the result, then nothing ever happens.

"Many people nowadays complain that meditation does not give them the expected results. But they forget the most important thing: you have to forget the result. Only then does anything happen. Tai Chi helps you be totally in the act. You forget the result. You practice and practice and practice. The more you practice, the sooner the result will happen.

"People must understand that the result is not immediate and it comes to you when you are totally immersed in the practice.

"There is no direct technique for enlightenment, my dear Rinchen," Karma Dorje concluded.

"So, do you mean that we use Tai Chi or any other form of meditation for enlightenment? I asked.

"Yes, meditation, Tai Chi or Qi Gong are tools that center us. They are the methods. The result is the enlightenment state. But remember: once you are centered, you are everywhere. Once you are centered, you are all over and you transform into the cosmic consciousness. The cosmic consciousness is everywhere. We rarely speak about the result -the enlightenment- because when we do a method, the result follows. If you know the method, if you know 'how', that will bring you to the result, to the 'what'.

"But what works for you is a personal matter. It could be one of the meditations we do here or Tai Chi or something else. The experience is always personal, dear Rinchen. If you do not feel you are centered, then you should change the method; you are not applying it properly. Centering is not the be-all and the end-all; it is just the path. And beyond all these methods, it is the personal experience. The Great Masters say that this experience is the reason why we are here: to enjoy it. Once the experience helps you center yourself, then all your energy will be focused there: in that center. But that center is too small for all the energy to be centered there. It will explode; the energy is too great for the center.

"So that is the reason why I say that, once you are centered, then you are everywhere. No center. Or you can say you are centered everywhere. In that moment, your energy is dissipated everywhere. One could say that, in a way, you 'die'.

"Great Masters have come here and all of them have said the same thing: you die and are reborn again in the same life. That happens when your energy explodes and you disperse all over. You are still in a human body, but you have conquered death. There is no time, nor energy; suddenly you are empty and the cosmic energy enters you. The pure energy comes inside you: this is a major transformation.

"Legend has it that, when Buddha died, all his close disciples were there beside him, crying. Buddha was very surprised and asked them why they were crying. And they looked at him and said 'Dear Master, you are dying. How can you ask such a question?'

"Buddha started laughing and said: 'You should have cried forty years ago. That is when I died, not now. Now you should be laughing. Be happy.'

"Beautiful, isn't it, dear Rinchen?" Karma Dorje smiled.

CHAPTER 4

The Method and the Master

W e were talking a few weeks ago about the difference between the method and the result; in our case we were talking about the method -the meditation or Tai Chi- and the result - the enlightenment. Is it possible to have a spontaneous result, a sudden enlightenment?" I asked Karma Dorje.

"Yes it is possible, dear Rinchen," Tenzin answered.

I had become used to the style of these Masters. It was as if only one person was speaking; not two. I felt like they were getting their answers from the same Source and they were part of that Source too.

I would often ask Tenzin Dhargey and Karma Dorje or Master Lama -Tenzin Tashi– a question and I felt that whoever answered, it would be the same. It was like they were all connected to an invisible library and they had access to any information they wanted too.

On the other hand, I could feel the other monks and intuitively I knew exactly who knew the answer. I could see that Tenzin Dhargey and Karma Dorje held a special status in the community of monks.

In a sense all the monks were equal, but when Tenzin Dhargey and Karma Dorje talked, the whole monastery listened. It took me a while to understand how lucky I was to have them with me almost every day for an hour or two.

"So, yes it is possible," Tenzin continued. "But it is very difficult. I know why you ask this question. Your mind is not interested in the method. Your mind is only interested in the result; in the outcome. And if you can bypass the method and go directly to the result, your mind will be very happy. Your mind clings to the result, dear Rinchen. Remember: I said *your mind*, not you.

"So that is the reason why you ask for a spontaneous enlightenment.

"Indeed, it is possible to achieve enlightenment effortlessly. But in order to achieve this 'effortlessly', you need to work a lot. You have to be ready for that spontaneous moment. You have to be purified inside; you have to be innocent, like a child. Look at a child and you will understand what it means to be spontaneous. Anything a child does, it is done without premeditation. It is done naturally. This is the reason that Jesus said that we have to become children again to enter Father's Kingdom. Jesus referred to spontaneity, to purity and to innocence. Jesus referred to a no-mind state.

"When I visited the United States and Europe, a lot of people asked me about the Zen path. They had heard about Zen's spontaneous enlightenment. And, of course, they wanted to reach the enlightenment state without any effort; without work, without meditation or Tai Chi, without anything. There, I noticed a tendency of the mind to calculate everything and try to place everything in a logical manner. But, because of the situation these people are in now, it is completely impossible.

All the belief patterns, all the preconceived opinions and artificiality make it impossible, dear Rinchen.

Methods are required to get rid of all of this. Enlightenment comes after you meditate, after experiences.

It is important for you to understand that all the methods you are learning here are extremely practical after the energy of the Earth changes. They are very good now too, but after 2012 they will be very effective, because the Mother Earth's energy will be completely different at that time."

"Are you telling me that twenty years from now, these methods are going to have maximum efficiency?" I asked stupefied.

"That is correct," Tenzin confirmed.

"These methods are ancient and very practical. However, because of specific astrological events that will happen at the end of 2012, they will be understood best from 2014 onwards. The energy will change from masculine to feminine. Therefore, people will be more open and the meditations will help them on their path of enlightenment. Until then, you have to practice them and master them. You received the initiation from us, so it will be easy for you to do it," Tenzin continued.

"Is it so important to receive an initiation? What about people who are not able to find a Master?" I asked.

"That is a good question, Rinchen," Karma Dorje answered.

"It is important to do something. If you read a meditation, a method that helps you be on a spiritual path, or if the method is explained to you, you can use it on your own. But nobody knows how much you will gain from the meditation, how it will work on you, what kind of energy you have, so on.

"It is better than nothing. However, when you work with a Master it is a different story. The Master selects a meditation; it is an individual approach.

"The meditation is not that important for the Master: you are important. The Master looks at all of you: your emotional aspect, your mental aspect, your level of consciousness, your actual life and past lives, so on. After that, the Master selects a particular meditation for you; a meditation that will change you, a meditation that fits you. In this case, the student must not speak to anybody about the method, because it is a personal meditation.

"Remember, dear Rinchen, each individual is unique and a different method must be given to each.

"These meditations that we do here are excellent tools for enlightenment; we use these methods for our Tibetan monks and they have all types of personalities that can be found in this world. Some of them in their past lives were in different countries doing different jobs, different things, so we know that the meditations are very practical.

"These meditations are specifically done to suit every personality, any individual in this world. Of course, one must practice them for a while to see if they suit them. One must find the right moment, when their energy and their body is ready to work with any of these meditations we are giving you or with a combination of them.

"When you go back there, one day you will remember all these meditations and you will share them with people around you to practice.

"At the same time, you will guide people to do some of these meditations and you will teach them to open their heart, to abandon their mind and their ego. When that happens, they will contact you directly. It might take months for them to be ready. You should explain to them what the right food is, how to sleep properly, what right living is. It will be a live relationship between you and them, a deep relationship."

"What can people out there achieve by practicing these meditations?" I asked him.

"They will go back to the source, their energy will reunite with the Universe; they will become formless. When you do that, you are practically immortal; not in the sense that you will be in this body forever, but in the sense that you will realize that you are not this body. You are a drop of the ocean; so you have the consciousness of the ocean, don't you?

Eventually these meditations will help people find their own source. They will stop being followers or imitators. They will become originals. You must be willing to lose it all before you can have it all. What does this mean? It means that until you are able to let go of everything, you will find it hard to hold onto anything. Detachment is the key. If you are too attached to something and are deeply unhappy without it, then you are not simply attached, you are addicted," Tenzin answered, smiling at me.

"What about love? I thought that love is also a form of meditation," I asked.

"Love is a door. A meditation or a method is a door too. Love is better than meditation because it is natural. Both love and meditation help you stay in the present. Your mind is canceled out.

"But if you open that door and you are *really* in love, you do not need a meditation; if you need a meditation, then something more is needed in this case.

"In pure love, nothing else is needed; the same applies to meditation. If you do a meditation correctly, then there is no need for something else. This very moment is eternity! There is no need for anything and there is no time; you are in the present.

"And remember, Rinchen: love does not mean sex, they way people think. Love does not mean possession or attachment to somebody or something. Love does not mean to feel lonely and be looking for somebody else, because you fear being alone.

"You can be in love with a flower or with a tree. You can be in love with the stars or the Sun or you can be in love with a waterfall, with Mother Earth. When you are in love, the presence of what you love becomes a meditative state. That is the reason why you do not need a meditation. Real love puts you in a non-thinking state. If you are with somebody that you think you are in love with and you are still thinking of them, then you are just two minds thinking. If you are really in love, your mind stops; nothing is needed. And people who love each other feel reverence for each other.

"When I was in the United States and in Europe, I was surprised to see how many couples told me that they are in love, but they were fighting all day. This is not love. In real love you find silence and peace. It is exactly like a meditation. The object of your love becomes sacred, divine. You are quiet, in silence. Why fight with your lover? What kind of love is this?

"Love must become devotion. In your world, Rinchen, love has become sex and a bodily thing, but when you are really in *love* it goes beyond sex; it becomes devotion. Only few people are able to reach devotion. Love is between the ravine, the canyon of sex and the infinite sky of devotion. You choose the direction in which to go: down or up.

"Why is the other person so important when you love? Because you are moving on the periphery and your lover becomes the center. On the other hand your lover sees you in the center and your lover sees herself or himself on the periphery. So, suddenly both of you are in the center.

"Both love and meditation set you free. Both meditation and love mean freedom. Ego is prison. Mind is prison. Once you are in love, the prison vanishes; it disappears. You will be under an open sky and you can fly.

"Love is not an action. You cannot 'build' love. Once you are in the process of 'building' love, an opposite will arise from this activity; the opposite of love is hate.

"That is why in these countries that I went to a few years ago, people go from one opposite to the other; they go from love to hate.

"The same person becomes the object of both love and hate. You are in a continuous fighting mood, in a continuous situation of conflict.

"I will show you how people can meditate when they love each other. And this meditation can be practiced at any time: in the kitchen when they see each other, in the living room, in the store when they go shopping or when they make love to each other.

"I will tell you about the **Love Meditation**. This meditation must be practiced by both lovers for five minutes, five hours, five days, five weeks or five months. Start first with five minutes and do it for one week.

"First step: feel reverence in the presence of your lover. See the divine in him or in her. Feel God in him or her. Make your relationship a sacred state.

"Second step: suddenly will feel that you are one and deep down a wall has broken. Your bodies cannot separate you; you become one in harmony and you completely forget that you are there.

"Try to do this meditation as many times as possible. It will change your life.

"Do not try to choose: should I meditate or should I love? Do both: love when you meditate and meditate when you love. Remember that love is a natural phenomenon. It is like breathing. Breathing is a vehicle that brings pure prana inside you. Love is a vehicle that brings pure divinity inside you. These vehicles, breathing and love, are natural phenomena. You do not need to force yourself to use them. You are naturally born like that: you need to breathe and you need to love. You do not need to think *'now I will breathe'* or *'now I will love'*. It is a normal and natural process. Just be aware of it and use it for your spiritual evolution", said Karma Dorje.

PART TWO

Mother Earth

To Ana Pricop, Karma Dorje and Tenzin Dhargey;
the Masters who first helped me remember who I really am.

CHAPTER 5

Connect with Earth's Energy

W hy do you keep your hands for over an hour every day on that tree?" I asked Karma Dorje one day, pointing at a small Himalayan yew that was growing in the monastery inside the court.

There were *Taxus Walliciana* trees inside and around the monastery. This elegant Himalayan yew is a medium-sized evergreen coniferous tree with thin and flat leaves arranged spirally on the shoots, but twisted at the base to appear in two horizontal ranks on all except for erect lead shoots. *Taxus Walliciana* is the source of the allopathic drug taxol, which is regarded as one of the most effective remedies for cancer.

"We are all in the hands and under the protection of Mother Earth as we were in our biological mother's womb," Karma answered inviting me to join Tenzin and him near the tree.

I placed my hands on the tree and, indeed, I felt the energy coming from below. It was like an invisible connection with Earth.

"Mother Earth energy gives us a vibration and a connection with Life that is vital for our survival," Tenzin explained.

"Without this energy, without this vibration, we would not be here. Our bodies come from Mother Earth. It is sort of a temporary 'rental' that we do, in order to manifest ourselves here.

"Each day we should connect with Mother Earth and meditate with Her. It is unfortunate that in the Western civilization people are so disconnected from Mother Earth," Tenzin continued.

I realized that both Masters were right.

I remember a lot of people living only in their houses, in their offices or inside of giant commercial centers and malls. People are completely disconnected from nature. Our daily activities cut us off almost completely from being in the middle of the nature. And even when we have a moment and we have time to stay surrounded by nature, we are still disconnected from Mother Earth; we just talk and talk or think continuously about our daily issues. We do not see much around us. We do not see the green grass or the flowers or the beautiful blue sky with white clouds.

"Is there a specific meditation that people could practice out there in order to get energy from Mother Earth? Is there a specific way to reconnect with Mother Earth?" I asked.

"Yes we will teach you this meditation, dear Rinchen, and in the future you will teach other people too. It is very important to do this meditation each morning and to connect with Mother Earth. We can say that this meditation is also a form of protection and grounding," Karma added.

"The correct meditation posture when you do the **Mother Earth Meditation** is to have your back straight and sit with legs crossed in a semi lotus posture, because of the energy flow increase on the superior level of chakras. It is also fine to sit on the edge of a chair with your back straight.

"So the first step is to keep a good meditation posture with a straight back and relaxed shoulders. Keep the tip of your tongue on the roof of the mouth, close your eyes and slightly cross them looking up towards the opening of your third eye. Start breathing all the way down to your navel area. Remember to move into the heart (the first step from Third Eye Meditation).

"The second step is to see yourself in the middle of nature and that you are becoming part of Mother Earth: you can feel, for example, that you become a flower or a tree: feel yourself grounded in the earth with strong and powerful roots that go deep down inside Mother Earth. Feel yourself actually becoming Earth herself. Inhale and feel that your body is part of the Divine Mother Earth. Feel that your breath is the same as Mother Earth's breath, your pulse is the same as Mother Earth's pulse; your heart is the same as Mother Earth's heart.

"Feel that you are earth. Feel that you are water. Feel that you are wood.

"Feel that you are fire. Feel that you are metal. Feel that you are earth, water, wood, fire and metal: the five elements of the Universe.

The third step is to feel that you are really big, as Mother Earth, and that you are orbiting around the Sun. You can feel Venus behind you and Mars in front of you. You can feel the whole Universe around you."

As Karma Dorje spoke, I could "*see*" the images of each step from the meditation. I could hear, but at the same time, I had images. It was almost like watching a movie accompanied by spoken commentaries.

I described this weird visual effect to the Masters.

"This is **Heart Imagery**, dear Rinchen," Tenzin replied.

I knew that *imagery*, in a literary text, is an author's use of vivid and descriptive language to add depth to their work. It appeals to human senses to deepen the reader's understanding of the work. There are seven types of imagery, each corresponding to a human sense, feeling, or action.

"I felt it like a sort of visual description of the language. I did not know that there is *Heart Imagery*," I told them.

"Yes, there is mind imagery and heart imagery. Heart imagery is more powerful, as it is connected with the subtle feminine energies of the heart. The heart has a powerful energy and anything that is created from that space has a completely different vibration compared with things or actions created from the mind. We will have time to discuss about this method later. We have a lot to say about it and work to do. Heart imagery contains dreaming and cleaning of dreams, cleaning the past, including reversing together with many other important techniques that help you harmonize your energies and understand the inter-dimensional activities more.

"The *Mother Earth Meditation* is very important," said Karma Dorje.

"A lot of people can clean themselves of physical and emotional problems if they connect with Mother Earth. This is the best way to balance yourself and harmonize your energies. It is also a way to reconnect with the entire Universe, through your Divine Mother."

* * *

I had studied the effect of walking barefoot or sitting with my hands on a tree and one of the most interesting books about this topic is *"Earthing: The Most Important Health Discovery Ever?"* written by Clint Ober, Stephen T. Sinatra and Martin Zucker.

The National Institute of Environmental Health Sciences in the US compiled a paper on the effects electromagnetic fields have on human health. The experiments made on animals were very interesting: these animals were not wearing shoes and sleeping in comfortable beds insulated from earth, they were naturally grounded. A herd of sheep sleeping under a power line, to study changes caused by electromagnetic fields in human melatonin levels.

Clint Ober came across a method to effectively ground people while in bed, to ground humans while asleep; the primary time when the healing and restoration of the body takes place.

The effort produced, with a control group, the following results:

85% went to sleep quicker.

93% reported sleeping better throughout the night.

100% reported waking, being and feeling more rested.

82% experienced a significant reduction in muscle stiffness.

74% experienced the elimination of/or a reduction of chronic back and joint pain.

78% reported improved general health.

In addition, some people in the study also reported experiencing significant relief from asthmatic and respiratory conditions, rheumatoid arthritis, PMS, sleep apnea and hypertension.

I would strongly encourage people to walk barefoot at least 20 minutes per day.

The effect is amazing. Clint Ober is right; the healing is right here, under our bare feet!

* * *

When I was a child, my cousins and I would walk barefoot each day on the dirt and I remember my grandma warming water for us to wash our feet each evening. One day one of my cousins told her, "Grandma, we're going to wear our shoes today. There's too much dirt on our feet." My grandma looked at him, smiled and said: "Oh, it's worth it."

Later, I understood that not only it is worth it, but it is **everything**. Literally everything; without this dirt and the barefoot exercise we are completely lost, disconnected, isolated and cut off from our reservoir of energy and vitality.

Anastasia, the Siberian Great Master, has said something even more important: if we create a connection with Mother Earth by working each day with Her, touching Her, taking care of her, speaking with Her, cleaning Her, sleeping outside and taking care of all that is connected with Her (plants, animals, fish and so on) we create a "space of love". In this "space of love" all that is there assists our evolution here on this planet.

A few years ago, I did the Anastasia "seeds experiment". I had kept each group of organic seeds under my tongue for nine minutes so that the seeds "would learn" my body's requests and needs. After that I planted them in my garden which I would take care of each day. I would spend at least four-five hours a day there. I would meditate there, talking to the earth, walking barefoot, giving love and energy to the seeds and to Mother Earth. When the tomatoes, green beans and green peppers would become ripe, I would sit there in the middle of the garden and eat them, being grateful for and appreciative of plants and Mother Earth.

Any health issue that I had at that time had completely disappeared. The plants had "learnt" my health problems and they had developed the necessary antidote just for my body, in order to heal it! I did indeed create a "space of love".

Anastasia was right: Mother Earth loves us beyond our understanding. She has given us everything including our bodies. Obviously we have biological parents, but we do have divine parents: divine Mother Earth and divine Father Universe (Sun).

However, the connection with Mother Earth begins inside of us. I have seen numerous people that preach about cleaning, caring and protecting Mother Earth, but they do the opposite. Mother Earth does not need that. She needs us to just be in our hearts and live in peace and love. Simple educative and learning acts for our children are good enough. The care of Mother Earth is supposed to be a normal, day to day activity. It is not something special. It is something natural.

There was a time when we were really connected with Mother Earth. We were so connected that everything came to us spontaneously and naturally.

Whenever I walk barefoot, meditate outside or do Tai Chi, I have a clear recollection of that time when we were in such harmony with the nature, with animals and birds, with everything around us: Mother Earth and Father Sky. And I really feel good. I remember what we really were: perfectly conscious of our acts, co-creators together with Divinity.

CHAPTER 6

The Inner Self

G od is connected with all of us through what we call the Inner Self. Some people call this connection the 'Higher Self'. Other people called it the 'Mind of God'. How this connection is made is beyond our understanding, but we do know that The Universal Father connects with every being through the Inner Self," Karma Dorje explained.

"The more we meditate, the more we increase the possibility to communicate with our Inner Self. One day, after years of meditation, we might be able to speak with our Inner Selves in the same way that we are speaking now, here; directly and naturally without any interference," added Tenzin Dhargey.

"Could you explain the difference between the Inner Self, the Spirit and the Soul a little bit more?" I asked the Masters.

"The Soul is like a library, dear Tenzin," said Karma Dorje.

"Our first manifestation as a being on any inhabited planet brings in something unique and personal: our Soul. Then, all our subsequent manifestations in different planes and dimensions bring more and more experiences to our Soul. There is a very well-known expression: 'an old soul'. That means that this person has had a lot of lives on different dimensions or a lot of lives and experiences here on this planet. Our Soul is like a universal vehicle that moves with all our experiences and information accumulated in our evolution.

"Our Spirit is our Consciousness or our Awareness, to put it in a different way. Our Spirit takes the final decision in our evolution. It is that part of us that is aware of each step we take. Our Spirit is not the same as our Inner Self. Our Spirit and our Soul personally belong to us and we will have them forever and ever.

"One could say that our Inner Self is 'prepersonal', meaning that it is beyond our Soul and Spirit. Our Inner Self has a distinctive and unique characteristic: it is God's manifestation in us. Basically when we connect with our Inner Self, we connect directly with God; you speak directly with God," Karma continued.

"You said something about the "Mind of God"; the Inner Self is also called the 'Mind of God'. Can you tell me more about it?" I asked curiously.

"Yes, in terms of mind, it is important to understand the distinction between the 'Real mind' or the 'Mind of God' and the reactive mind or our daily thoughts. First you have to understand that the mind is not in the brain as so many people believe. The mind is outside the brain. The mind is not produced by brain.

"The mind or the sum of your thoughts can be divided into three parts:

- ❖ The Reactive Mind
- ❖ The Real Mind
- ❖ The Decision Factor or The Observer

"What is the **Reactive Mind**? Reactive mind characteristics:

- ❖ It produces thoughts related either to the past or the future; not to the present.
- ❖ It produces thoughts of superiority and dominance.
- ❖ It likes to criticize people around it.
- ❖ It loves to condemn actions around it.
- ❖ It produces resentments; it usually likes to attack.
- ❖ It loves to complain about anything.
- ❖ It likes to label anything and anybody: good/bad, stupid/ smart, beautiful/ugly, friend/enemy.

What is the **Real Mind**? Real Mind characteristics:

- ❖ It only produces thoughts related to the present.
- ❖ It is based on neutral thoughts: basically you are an observer not a judge.

❖ It does not judge or condemn anyone or anything.

❖ It is free of conflict; it does not create a conflict with another mind; basically when we do that, we only strengthen the power of the conflict in our own mind.

❖ It does not put us in a 'role'; does not condition us.

❖ It keeps us keen and alert; it gives total vigilance: we live in the present, our mind does not fly. This increases our energetic field vibration tenfold; the field which gives life to our body

What is the **Decision Factor** or the **Observer**?

Our Decision Factor or Observer is the power to verify our own thoughts and change them; 99% of us have a decision factor in sleep mode. Before moving from the reactive mind to the real mind, we need to pass through our Observer. There, we decide whether to go back to the reactive mind or to the real mind.

The Observer is similar to the *Void* that exists when we move from one dimension to another.

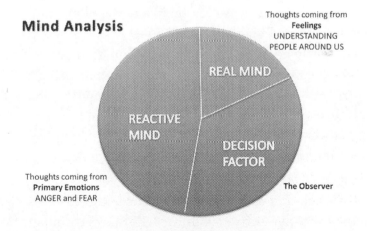

Sometimes when we connect with your real mind or Inner Self, we don't have any thoughts. We are completely empty and free of any ideas and concepts. In that instant, we can really communicate with God; we can ask any question and we will get an answer.

"How can we contact our Inner Self" I asked curiously.

"Well, we are already doing that in an unconscious way each moment of our existence. Sometimes we call our Inner Self *'intuition'* or *'the inner voice'*. The question is how we can contact out higher self in a conscious way. There is a specific meditation: The **Inner Self Meditation**. The Inner Self Meditation is easy to do and has an immediate effect if you do it right and you contact your own mind of God.

"The first step is to keep a good meditation posture with a straight back and relaxed shoulders. Keep the tip of your tongue on the roof of the mouth, close your eyes and slightly cross them looking up towards the opening of your third eye. Start breathing all the way down to your navel area. Remember to move into the heart (the first step from the Third Eye meditation). Again, feel the vibration of the Divine Mother Earth. With your intention move your Spirit inside your heart and, with your inner vision, see two sacred, tranquil and serene mountains in front of you. Between the mountains there is a beautiful waterfall. At the bottom of the mountains is a meadow with flowers and birds; it is like paradise.

"Sit there with your legs crossed in a perfect lotus posture and relax your mind and body. When you feel ready to call you Inner Self, do it gently and use all your intention. Your Inner Self will come to you in any form possible: it may be a human being, an angel, a thought, a ray of light, a celestial being, a geometrical form like a pyramid, a crystal; anything.

"Your Inner Self is always full of love and compassion; it is the representation and the reflection of the Divine Wisdom and Divine Knowledge. Ask your Inner Self what you must do to get out of spiritual isolation and to increase your level of consciousness. Remember that answer from your Inner Self; feel the magnificence of this meeting. Feel the splendor and the radiance coming from this holy communication." And with that, Tenzin ended his speech, looking into my eyes with a big smile.

* * *

"How can we have a perfectly healthy body and mind?" I asked my Tibetan Masters.

"Health is a relative thing, my dear Rinchen. The body cannot be perfectly healthy. If you were to have a perfectly healthy body, you would not die; ever.

"Here, and according to the Eastern spiritual systems, we consider the mind itself a disease. We never say: *a perfectly healthy body and mind'*, as this is absurd. First of all, the body will die, sooner or later. So health can only be a relative thing.

"The body is only in a relative balance. Death and life are part of our existence and death progresses with life every moment. The day we are born, we begin the dying process. It is not an option. If we are in the process of dying every moment, how can we really be healthy? We are relatively healthy. So it is sufficient to say that we are *'normally healthy'*, not *'perfectly healthy.'*

"The same applies to the mind. The very nature of mind is that we are not perfectly healthy: thinking means that we are relatively healthy; it is the same, as it is with the body.

"The mind is a bridge between body and spirit. When we think, we connect with the body. When we meditate and we do not think, we connect with the spirit. This continuous link between body and spirit, between matter and non-matter, between dying and non-dying, keeps the mind in a constant rigid, stretched and stiff status. Moving from visible to invisible is not easy. So in fact, mind is an action, a process. Mind is not a thing. Mind is an activity, an operation, an exercise.

"I used to teach meditation in some of the Western countries. They would get upset and ask me why they were becoming so worried, so tense during meditation. I explained that this is not because of meditation. The process of meditation was helping them become conscious of their thoughts. Thoughts are with us every moment, but because we are so occupied with our external activities we are not aware of our thoughts. When we meditate our thoughts rush, they come to us and we feel this inner tension, inner violence inside of us. So mind is an effort; energy is used and the more we think the larger quantity of energy is used. I have met people that do not do any physical effort; they just think all day long and are exhausted, drained of their energy and very tired.

"So there is no such thing as a *'perfectly healthy mind'*. Your question does not make sense. We are born pure, directly connected with the Spirit; without mind. Parents, schools and society have trained us to have a mind. We are born with no mind. At that early stage, the mind is just a potentiality; it is just something in the future. We are conditioned over time by others for certain purposes and the mind appears; it is born. The mind always holds us to the past or it tries to build a future. There is no such a thing as *the present* for the mind. The mind is a box. All these Zen stories that tell us to *'get out of the box'* refer to the mind.

"When I visited the Western countries, I was surprised by the magnitude of importance people place on the mind. They have even developed a science of mind: psychology. We, here in Eastern side of the world, do not care much about mind, about this box. We are interested in finding ways to get out of the box. We look for an exit, for a door, for something that helps us get out of the box.

"This is the only reason why we talk about mind. We try to go beyond it. And once we manage to get out of the box, we can *see*. We can see the great infinite universe. And we start laughing when we see how stupid we had been until we got out of the box, out of the mind. We had been thinking that the Universe is there in that small box, that ignorant mind. Once we move out into the open sky, once we have the impact with the infinite universe, we become *conscious*. We are not prisoners in that box anymore.

"As long as people think that the infinite universe is in the box, then they are prisoners. They are limited; they do not comprehend God. They do not comprehend that God is beginning-less, timeless, space-less and endless. How can they comprehend the Infinite when they are confined in a limited space?" Tenzin concluded.

"Is it possible to get out of the box?" I asked looking at both Masters.

"Yes, of course, it is possible. There are limitless methods. Some of them are unknown to humans. One of the best is the **'STOP'** method. If you can stop yourself when your mind is in the middle of the process, then you are out of the box. It is easy when you do it without any premeditation. Do not program yourself to stop in the middle of thinking. Of course, it would be better if you had a friend say '*STOP*' without warning and so you would have to stop immediately from whatever it is that you are doing.

"You need to stop thinking, to stop working. You even need to stop breathing.

"But remember that it needs to be authentic: if it is not authentic it will not work. And the simple way is to start reducing your repetitive habits. If you habitually tend to use a word, a gesture or a particular phrase, you need to drop it. Any habit that is stopped suddenly brings inner silence and it quietens your mind.

"For example, if you tend to nod your head when you say a sentence, and you do it in order to emphasize your words, then try to say the words without nodding your head. If you can do that, then suddenly you will feel a certain freedom, a certain veil lifting from your eyes. Any mechanical response should be stopped; a mechanical response, a habit is a trick of the mind. If you can break down these habits, then the mind disappears for a moment and you will be able to *see*. It is easy, but you need to persevere; you need to repeat this method as many times as possible," Karma Dorje explained.

"There is another method to stop the thinking process and get out of the box," Tenzin added.

"There is a meditation, which we call '**The Statue Meditation**'. It is a very simple and effective way to get out of the mind's trap. You basically see yourself becoming a statue; heavy, solid, dense like a stone.

"The first step is to close your eyes and relax your entire body. You can do this by sitting in a chair or lying down.

"The second step is to feel that you are just a stone; you cannot move at all. You are like a statue. You cannot move your hands; you cannot open your eyes. Any pain you have in your body disappears. You are like dead. Suddenly everything around you will disappear: the chair or the bed, the room, the whole world will vanish. You will become centered in yourself and your mind will have stopped.

"If you do this meditation correctly then you will be able to get out of the box. Try it tonight and you will see," Tenzin smiled.

CHAPTER 7

Eating Healthily

I have noticed that you do not eat much; almost nothing. And you have a very short list of vegetables on your menu," I observed one day.

"That is true; eating for us is not the most important activity," said Karma Dorje.

"From our studies we know that the human liver cannot process more than four elements. It is like overworking it until it reaches exhaustion. If you eat more than four elements, your liver gets burned out. For example, a simple piece of bread has at least four elements: water, yeast, flour and salt. In the western countries, they also add other ingredients in bread, such as sugar and baking powder. It literally pushes your liver to exhaustion when you eat more than four elements.

"That is the reason why we usually just have some boiled rice or some tea. That is sufficient for us; and it is very healthy at the same time. Also we love to have some vegetables on the table, but we do not exaggerate.

"There is a reason why, in all spiritual traditions, people fast before a celebration or a ceremony. They wish to purify their bodies and spirit beforehand.

"But the most important thing is how we combine our food. Why? Because it helps one to fully digest. If food enters your intestines incompletely digested, it builds putrefaction inside your organism, which stays blocked there for years. As a result, you have a constant source of *toxic substances* inside you, which poison you every day. They expose you to many diseases and develop an excellent environment for harmful bacteria and intestinal parasites.

"Mucous plaque also forms and that can stay in the intestines for up to 10 years. However, it can usually be eliminated via detoxification methods (vegetable fibers or diuretic tea).

"All these things expose you to many diseases such as cancer, skin diseases, digestive diseases and constipation.

"If you combine food in the wrong way for more than 10 years, your body definitely becomes sick. What really happens in the stomach? When food enters the stomach, the gastric juice adjusts its acidity and enzymes, so that the food can be completely digested. Eating two types of food together, which require different adjustments of the gastric juice, results in a gastric juice that does not completely digest either type of food.

"Food enters into the intestine incompletely digested and becomes putrefied. The result is accumulation of toxic substances in the intestine. Some organs (i.e., the liver, the pancreas and the kidneys) get sick. This leads to a chronic disease.

"Now there is a new way of eating in the western countries: organic or non-organic. I was amazed to find out that you have to pay more, in order to eat healthily; you have to buy organic food. It is as if the governments of the countries are aware of unhealthy food and they agree to their people not having unhealthy food.

"If this is the future of humanity, then we will have a lot of problems!

"However, all these chronic diseases can happen even if we eat organic food and we combine it in the wrong way.

"Let me explain some of the Food Combination Rules. I will try to describe the best (or optimum) combinations, the neutral combinations and the harmful combinations.

"I studied how people eat, especially in the United States and in the western part of Europe, and tried to gather all the information together.

"I know that in the western countries, people do not take food combination much into consideration; but, in fact, this is the most important thing. I noticed that people consider that combining ten ingredients together is good and that it is a sign of prosperity, but, in fact, they destroy their own bodies day after day if they continue with this pattern.

"There were many times when I was invited to dinner. People should understand that eating in the evening is very harmful for their liver. The most important meal is in the morning: breakfast. At lunch we should eat less than half of what we have eaten in the morning and in the evening we should just have tea or some water.

"So let us see the *food combination rules*.

Eggs should never be combined with fish or meat. There is a risk if combined with cheese, wheat starch products (bread, pasta, potatoes, rice, corn) and nuts or seeds.
Eggs go very well with fresh vegetables.

Meat should never be combined with fish, eggs, cheese or wheat starch products.
There is a risk if combined with nuts and seeds.
Meat goes very well just with fresh vegetables.

Fish should never be combined with eggs, meat and cheese.
There is a risk if combined with nuts and seeds.
Fish goes very well with fresh vegetables and wheat starch products.

Cheese should never be combined with fish and meat.
There is a risk if combined with eggs.
Cheese goes very well with fresh vegetables, wheat starch products, nuts and seeds.

Wheat starch products should never be combined with meat.
There is a risk if combined with eggs.

Wheat starch products go very well with fresh vegetables, cheese, fish, nuts and seeds.

Fresh vegetables go well with any product.

Fruit goes alone; it is not combined with anything. Fruit alone constitutes a meal!

"**What happens when we have a 'No' combination**? Firstly, the stomach cannot digest two concentrated types of food (concentrated food means any food that is not a raw vegetable or fruit). Also, we should never combine meat with eggs and cheese and we should never combine animal protein (meat, cheese, eggs) with pasta, bread, potatoes, rice or pastries. Therefore, avoid combining french fries with steak, or pasta with meat.

"You should never combine fruit and sweets (sugar) with any type of food. A fruit must be eaten on an empty stomach, one hour before the meal or at least two hours later. Sugar, honey or fructose inhibits gastric secretion and by combining them with the rest of the food, you feel very uncomfortable after the meal.

"Avoid combining fatty foods (butter, cream, oil) with those that are rich in proteins or starch.

"And another very important thing: avoid drinking water during or after a meal. It dilutes the gastric juices and the digestion is very poor. Water must be drunk at least 20-30 minutes before meals. Milk or melon must not be combined with any other food. Do not consume acids and sweet fruit at the same time.

"Acid fruits can be combined together (oranges, apple, and berries). Sweet fruit must be eaten separately (only bananas or only pears).

"What is a good combination? A good combination of proteins must be combined with vegetables that are low in starch, especially the green ones (parsley, spinach, tomatoes, cucumbers, green pepper, broccoli, cabbage). Fatty food can be combined with light vegetables.

"Pasta, potatoes, bread, corn and rice can be combined with beans, peas, lentil, and chickpeas. Eat only fruit or drink only milk on an empty stomach.

"Any types of sweets must be eaten only on an empty stomach. So, give up the dessert after the meals. Dessert is a very unhealthy habit. It is better to just continue eating food rather than having dessert. If you still feel the desire to have desert after a meal, it means you did not give your body the food it really needed.

"The desire to eat certain food is very powerful. In the United States, I saw people getting out of the house at midnight to buy some chocolate or sandwiches or something else! This strong feeling of wanting something to eat indicates two things: either that the emotional body is not harmonized and not balanced or that the body is missing an ingredient from that food that they are longing for.

"It is interesting to analyze these desires.

"If you are always hungry, then you need tyrosine, which can be found especially in oranges, lemons, vegetables and red fruits or you need tryptophan which can be found in cheese, spinach, potatoes or raisins.

"If you always want to eat salty food, then you need to have some goat milk, fish or natural sea salt.

"If you are longing for something sweet, then you need chromium which can be found in fresh fruits, cheese, beans or you need phosphorus which can be found in eggs, spinach, raisins, potatoes or dairy products.

"If you are craving for chocolate then you need magnesium that which can be found in nuts, seeds, fruits and vegetables.

"If you are addicted to coffee or tea then you need sulphur and iron that can be found in eggs, garlic, onion, salt, fish, herbs and vegetables.

"If you need to drink liquids, remember that you need at least eight glasses of water per day. We are made up of almost 70% water, so do not neglect water; it is very important for the human body. Unfortunately, people do not drink natural spring water anymore, which is alive. They drive to the supermarket and buy the bottled water, which does not have any life in it and it is filled with chlorine and other chemicals.

"If you do not want to eat, then you need vitamins B1 and B3 that can be found in beans, nuts and seeds, fish and vegetables." And with that, Tenzin ended his lecture on the combination of food.

* * *

Later, after I had returned from Tibet, I studied the effect of energy on water and I would strongly recommend the work of Dr. Masaru Emoto for all those interested in this subject.

Dr. Masaru Emoto is a Japanese energy scholar best known for his claims that human consciousness has an effect on the molecular and chemical structure of water.

Emoto's ideas are presented in the documentary *"What the Bleep Do We Know!"*

CHAPTER 8

The Sixth Sense

W hy is it so important to meditate in darkness? I have noticed that when I was meditating during that week up in the mountain rooms, you asked me to stay only in the farthest room where no light could enter," I asked very curiously.

"Darkness is very important in the evolution of any spiritual person," Karma Dorje answered.

"We live in a world of polarities where light and dark have the same intensity, the same energy. We should not fear darkness. We should feel the energy, regardless of its manifestation: light or dark. We should love darkness as much as we love light and remember that darkness is outside and inside of us.

"While in the United States, I heard that modern physicists have studied the behavior of the Universe and they demonstrated that all this darkness around the planets and galaxies is energy, nothing else: pure energy.

"We use darkness in our meditation for a couple of reasons.

"First, darkness is deeply relaxing. Try to mediate in the light and then in darkness. You will feel the difference immediately. In darkness, with nothing to be seen, your eyes usually stop all movement and they relax. Then you can center yourself pretty easily. If you meditate in the light, even if your eyes are closed, sometimes you may feel a tension there. When you are in darkness, your eyes relax. And when your eyes relax you can see your inner light. All of us have the inner light."

The Inner Light Meditation

The first step is to either go into a dark room and close your eyes or simply cover your eyes with a sleeping mask. Be sure there is no light coming in.

When your face has completely relaxed, "look" around and within, keeping your eyes closed, and without moving either head or eyes. Imagine yourself in the middle of darkness. See, sense and feel the darkness; feel it inside of you. Darkness will deeply relax you. Darkness will be outside and inside of you. Feel and love the darkness, as you do this exercise.

Suddenly, in the middle of this darkness, a light will appear.

"This is a very good meditation to understand that light and darkness are the same. While doing this meditation, feel the darkness, love the darkness.

"After a while you will feel that you cannot move at all; you will feel that you are like a statue. Your eyes will stop moving and the energy inside you will split and move towards three directions: down into the navel area, into the middle of the heart area and up into the third eye. It is like a river of fire that splits into three directions.

"You might feel your first sphere of energy - the navel sphere – fill with fire, vigor and vitality.

"Or you might feel that your heart sphere begins to vibrate and pulsate.

"Or you might really feel the energy going up to the third eye. You will feel a heat, a flow of fire - a liquid flame trying to find a new path, a new route.

"Welcome anything that occurs. Do not be afraid. Cooperate with the energy; let it be.

"The next thing that will occur, regardless of where the energy moves to (navel, heart or third eye), is that darkness will disappear and there will be light. There will be light without a source. This is the original light, the holy light.

"We are used to seeing light that comes from a source. That source may be the sun, a lamp, the moon or something else. There is always a source.

"However, when the energy moves towards one of these three centers (navel, heart or third eye) you will see a light that does not have a source. The light is there, inside of you; it does not come from an outside source. The energy assists the veil of darkness to display the light. We call it *'God's light'* because God's light is eternal and source-less. This is the original light; all scriptures and holy books make reference to this light.

"Sometimes you will need to stay and meditate for some time before the energy moves towards one of the three centers and you are able to see the original light. When you see the original light, you will go through a transformation. And this is not simply imagination: it is really a light, a complete light, without end or boundaries.

"It is perfect light; this light goes all over without producing any effects, as the sun light does, such as shadow or heat."

*   *   *

It is interesting to notice that all over the world, indigenous ethnic groups (native tribes, such as the Kogi, the Mayans, the Arhuaco, e.t.c.), do extensive meditations in darkness.

Up in the Sierra Mountains of Colombia, the Kogi who are descendants of the Tairona culture that had flourished before the Spanish conquest, meditate in darkness. The Tairona were an advanced civilization which built many stone structures and pathways in the jungles.

The Kogi call the Pico Cristóbal Colón Mountain (the highest mountain in Colombia with an estimated height of 5,700 meters) *"Gonawindua"*, the Holy Mountain. There, the Kogi Masters, known as Mamas (which means "the sun" in Kogi), undergo strict training to become Great Masters. Male children are selected from birth and taken to a dark cave for the first nine years of their lives to begin this training. In the cave, elder Mamas, including the mother, care for, feed, train and teach the boys to attune to *"Aluna"* before they go back to the outside world. Through deep meditation and divination, the Mamas support the balance of harmony and creativity in the world. All their meditations are carried out in the caves of *"Gonawindua,"* the Holy Mountain, where they meditate in darkness.

After my week in darkness in Tibet (see *"Circles without Centers"*) I attended an extraordinary spiritual event: the Dark Room Retreat in Thailand with a group of around forty-five people in complete darkness and without food for approximately ten days. We practiced different meditations and, although we had no food, we really enjoyed it. Somewhere on the third or fourth day, we began to *see the original light*. And this light came from within us. It was amazing. We realized how the Masters are able to *see* in darkness.

*   *   *

"The Inner Light Meditation is a great way to see your inner light," said Karma Dorje.

"An interesting particularity of the inner light, when you see it, is that it does not produce any shadow. There is light everywhere; there is no source or receiver, as happens with daily sunlight or during evenings when we light candles.

"The inner light is a sixth sense.

"Another sixth sense is given by inner vibration. To achieve inner vibration, meditation has to be carried out for a longer period of time. I will guide you through it step by step. Once you manage to do this, it will become easy.

"This meditation has to be done 3 times, 9 times, 27 times, 54 times or 108 times. Of course, start at the beginning with 3 times."

Inner Vibration Meditation

Move into the Heart and keep the tongue touching the roof of the mouth

Send your love to Mother Earth.

❖ Visualize the five main chakras: the perineum chakra, the navel chakra, the heart chakra, the third eye chakra, the crown chakra; Go to each of them and feel them; each chakra has a *feeling*, a sensation; it provides a specific perception. When you do this exercise, visualize at each chakra the image and the energy of a Master whom you know and love. Stay at each chakra for just 2-3 seconds. Feel it and see the image of the Master. After you arrive at the crown chakra, go back to the first chakra using the backward route: fifth chakra, fourth, third, second and first. When you do the backward route, see, sense and feel the Masters again in each chakra.

❖ Start breathing down to the first chakra; the perineum chakra. Inhale normally, but give out a long and slow exhalation. After that, stay for 3-4 seconds in that time when you are in between the exhalation and the next inhalation. Do this exercise three times. There is a specific way to inhale for the first chakra. It is as if you are filling a bottle with water. Try to visualize that the flow of air, which is brought through your nostrils, is going down to the first chakra. Do this three times.

❖ Move your attention to the second chakra; the navel chakra. Follow the same procedure as with the first chakra: inhale normally, but give out a long and slow exhalation. After that, stay for 3-4 seconds in that time when you are in between the exhalation and the next inhalation. Do this three times. There is a specific way to inhale for the second chakra. It is the same as with the first chakra: as if you are pouring water into a bottle. Try to visualize that the flow of air, which is brought through your nostrils, is going down to the navel chakra. Do this three times.

❖ Move your attention to the third chakra: the heart chakra, in the middle of your chest area. Follow the same procedure as with the first two chakras. Do this three times.

❖ Move your attention to the fourth chakra: the third eye chakra in the middle of your forehead. Follow the same procedure as with the first three chakras, but now, breathe in to the third eye: see, sense and feel that the flow of prana is going from the nostrils directly to the third eye. Do this three times.

❖ Move your attention to the fifth chakra: the crown chakra, right on top of your head, where the fontanel is. Follow the same procedure as with the other four chakras.

❖ See, sense and feel that the flow of prana is going from the nostrils directly to the third eye. Do this three times.

❖ Go back now from the fifth chakra down to the first chakra, following the same breathing technique.

❖ Place one palm over the other (males place their right palm over the left and females place their left palm over the right) and place them on the navel. Start doing gently anti-clockwise circles over it. Do this 27 times.

❖ Now put your palms over your chest and do the same exercise for the heart center.

❖ Then, place your palms over the middle of your forehead and do the same exercise for the third eye center.

❖ Stay there for a few minutes and feel the three centers vibrate (navel, heart and third eye).

"This is a meditation that might take more time. Once you set yourself in the process of doing this meditation, it becomes a very powerful experience. We used to say that, when done 3 times in a meditation, we receive energy and attain stamina for the whole day; when done 9 times in a meditation, we receive energy for the whole month; when done 27 times in a meditation, our body never gets sick; when done 54 times, our body becomes light and when done 108 times, we become immortal," and with that Karma Dorje concluded his teachings.

While doing this meditation, for the first chakra I would effortlessly visualize the image and energy of Mother Mary; for the second chakra I would see Buddha. For the third chakra I would visualize Archangel Michael, for the fourth chakra I would see Babaji and for the crown chakra I would see Jesus.

Mother Mary: *First Chakra*: Earth Chakra, EXISTENCE
Buddha: *Second Chakra*: Navel Chakra, BEING
Archangel Michael: *Third Chakra*: Heart Chakra, FEELING
Babaji: *Fourth Chakra*: Third eye Chakra, KNOWLEDGE
Jesus: *Fifth Chakra*: Crown Chakra, DIVINITY

Visit
www.danielmitel.com/inner-vibration-meditation-masters
*to see the Inner Vibration Meditation Masters
as Daniel sees Them in his meditations*

I found this meditation so powerful, that I still do it now. It is very easy to move the consciousness from one chakra to another. After I have done 27 circles over the navel, heart chakra and third eye chakra, I feel the vibration. I literally feel my body vibrating and I feel the energy moving within it. I can feel the vibration of each center (navel, heart and third eye). I feel the inner vibration.

PART THREE

Dreaming &
Cleaning the Past

*To all the Masters and Light Workers who have never given up on us
and who have helped us find the path again towards Divinity.*

CHAPTER 9

Dreaming

I remember when you talked about dreams during the first days of our encounter; you said that we continuously dream; night and day. You said that only a few people in this world are awake. What does that mean?" I asked the Masters.

"Indeed, we dream all the time; we are constantly dreaming. People believe that we dream only when we are asleep, but that is not true; we dream during the day too," Tenzin Dhargey replied.

"During our meditations and especially during your dark room meditation and your meeting with our Lama Master Tenzin Tashi, I am sure that you experienced some awakening stages," Karma Dorje remarked.

"The dream is still there in you, even if you have concealed it with your daily activities. If you close your eyes and relax your body for a few seconds, you can feel that the dreams are there; you can feel that you are still in a dream," Karma Dorje added.

I probably looked dumb, because both Masters started laughing.

"I have been having a hard time believing that we are all dreaming now. How can that be possible?" I asked skeptically.

"How do you differentiate last night's dreams from now? How do you know you are not in a dream? How do you differentiate dreams from the 'real' world?" Tenzin Dhargey asked me.

"That is easy; I can touch you, I can see you and feel you. I know that I am awake," I answered and I touched Tenzin Dhargey's hand to show him what I meant.

"Well, that is exactly the point: there is no difference between your dreams and your 'reality'. Let us do an experiment; let us take a nap, the three of us," Karma Dorje suggested.

I agreed and lay down on the small bed behind me; the Masters remained in the same posture (the lotus posture). They just closed their eyes and I could feel that they had instantly fallen asleep.

I still wonder how they had fallen asleep so quickly. I was instantly projected into a dream. Both Masters were there. Tenzin Dhargey asked me to touch his hand. I did so and I instantly knew that we were dreaming.

This does not happen very often, for me to be aware that I am dreaming, but, at that moment, I was able to know that we were dreaming.

I opened my eyes. The Masters were waiting patiently for me.

"So do you now feel any difference between touching me in the dream and touching me before taking this nap?" Tenzin Dhargey asked smiling.

"Not really," I mumbled almost ashamed by this discovery.

"So do you understand what is going on now? It is not that you dream when you are asleep; it is that, in your sleep, you can feel dreams easily because your daily activities are not there.

"When you get up in the morning the dreaming continues inside while you *start acting on the outside* and the whole activity, the whole daily activity, covers and suppresses the dreaming.

"The dreams are always there, inside of you; the dreaming continues and you are not really awake. You are less asleep during the day because of your activities. Dreaming creates a film, a movie, a motion picture over the consciousness; it is like a fog.

"While we are asleep during the night, we are just relatively more asleep; during the day we are less asleep! You can say that you are really awake when there is no dreaming at all, isn't it so?" Tenzin Dhargey asked.

"Yes, I guess so. Basically we have to stop the *inner dreaming*, in order to really be awake," I answered surprised by the truth and common sense of the Masters' explanation.

"That is precisely and exactly what we should do, dear Tenzin," Karma Dorje said.

"There is no dream inside! Inside, it is just pure consciousness; a non-dreaming consciousness. This non-dreaming consciousness is the *awakening* or the *enlightenment*. All the scriptures and holy books say the same thing: we are asleep and we have to awaken," Tenzin Dhargey added.

"So, basically, we do not have a clue who we really are; it is like we are drunk all the time!" I exclaimed.

"Exactly; it is as if you are continuously watching a movie. The movie is projected onto the screen and you are so absorbed by it that the only thing you understand now is the movie, the story of the movie. You have completely forgotten who you really are; you are confused and you identify yourself with the actors from the movie, instead of seeing yourself as the spirit, the consciousness that *is watching* the movie.

"Dreaming is just a movie; dreaming is your mind reflecting the world. You have become so involved in it; you have identified yourself so much with it that you have completely forgotten who you really are.

"It is funny how that works: you see everything except yourself. This self-ignorance is dreaming; it is sleeping.

"While in the United States, I noticed that people would watch evening movies at home. One member of the family, who had invited and accommodated me there, was very surprised that I did not join them to watch a movie every evening. I only meditated. However, one evening I decided to accept their invitation and join them.

"They offered a nice and comfortable armchair for me to sit on, but I preferred to sit on the floor with a small pillow under my buttocks. All the family sat around me to watch the movie.

"I do not remember exactly what the whole movie was about, but it told the story of a young girl and a boy who had fallen in love and the girl's parents did not approve of this passionate love.

"It was just a movie, a story. During these two hours, though, the whole family was reduced to tears. They were weeping for two hours, since, to them, the movie was a tragedy. To me, it was nonsense. It was just a movie; a story. For two hours, this family was not even there. Basically they had identified themselves with the actors.

"When the movie ended, they started laughing over how they had cried during the movie and they were teasing each other.

"Well, that is how our life is: a movie that continuously runs, but it does not last for two hours. This dreaming situation runs for hundreds of lives; hundreds of lives lost in dreaming!" Tenzin Dhargey concluded.

* * *

"That is depressing; we are continuously dreaming!" I was somewhat disturbed by this realization.

"These are not just dreams, dear Tenzin. For you and for the rest of the people, they are *the reality*; your reality and their reality!" Karma Dorje replied with a warm smile.

"What happens if the dreams suddenly disappear?" I asked the Masters very curiously.

Masters Tenzin Dhargey and Karma Dorje exchanged a quick glance and they suddenly became very serious. I sensed that my question was very important and they were trying to answer it in a way that I would understand.

"If this world would suddenly disappear, it would be a very powerful shock, dear Tenzin. You could easily die from this shock; your world is your dreaming.

"I mean, what you see as 'the world' is not made up of external things, but of our dreams. Everyone lives in their own dream world; each mind is a world of dreaming. When more minds have the same dream, this is the result: the world you 'see' now.

"Without dreams, it might be very difficult for people to live. That is why we have meditations to gradually see that we are dreaming.

"There are indeed some quick methods - Zen is one of the most well known paths of sudden enlightenment - but generally you should avoid a sudden jump into the Eternity.

"You could do, it because there is no obstacle; there has never been any obstacle to a sudden realization, but it can be dangerous. It might be too much for you, because you are accustomed and adapted only to the dreaming world; you cannot face reality," Karma Dorje explained.

"Is there a method that could help us get out of this deep sleep; to transcend and go beyond the dreaming stage?" I asked the Masters.

"The best method is to start behaving as if the whole world is just a dream. We call this the '**This is Just a Dream Exercise**' method.

"It is very simple and effective. Whatever you do, remember this is just a dream. While you eat, walk, read or watch something, say to yourself: '*this is a dream*'. While you are awake, allow your mind to remember, without interruption, that everything, all that exists around you, is a dream.

"This meditation eventually helps you become aware within your dreams, during the night sleep, that this is a dream. If, while dreaming, you wish to remember that you are dreaming, start while you are awake. When you dream, you cannot remember that you are in a dream; you believe that what you see is your reality.

"If you see me here and then you close your eyes and go into a dream and see me in your dream, there will be no difference. You can even touch me and, still, there will be no difference.

"Remember the experiment we did a few hours earlier, when you could not make out the difference between touching me while awake and touching me while you were asleep?

"What you saw in both cases was just a picture mirrored in your eyes. In your eyes there is just a reflection of me. And it is a three-dimensional reflection, regardless of whether you see me now or in your dreams while you are asleep.

"So when you do the 'This is Just a Dream Exercise' method, do not try to change the dream, because if you do, you emphasize the dream and the effort to change the dream is falsely based on the belief that the dream is real.

"You only need to constantly and continuously remember, for a period of three months, that whatever you do, it is just a dream. If you can do this for three months straight, then the old pattern of the mind will begin to dissolve.

"If you can constantly awaken yourself and remind yourself continuously that '*this is a dream*' for three consecutive months, then one night during the fourth month, while you are dreaming, you will suddenly remember that 'this is a dream'.

"This is a very powerful tool to destroy the dreaming process; to remain aware, vigilant and conscious all the time.

"When you see a car, say: '*this is a dream*'. While slicing bread in the morning, say: '*this is a dream*'. While cleaning your house say: '*this is a dream*'. While working say: '*this is a dream*'," Tenzin Dhargey explained.

CHAPTER 10

Cleaning the Past

W hy do our memories sometimes trigger in us a powerful emotional response? Why does our past haunt us?" I asked the Masters.

"It has to do with the energy that you lost in past incidents. It is also related to other people's energy, which has been retained within you. Around your physical body is a perfect sphere of energy that keeps all these 'foreign' energies that others have left within your emotional body. With the passing of time, years, this energy becomes a burden. When this sphere is clean you can see, sense and feel all things around you very easily.

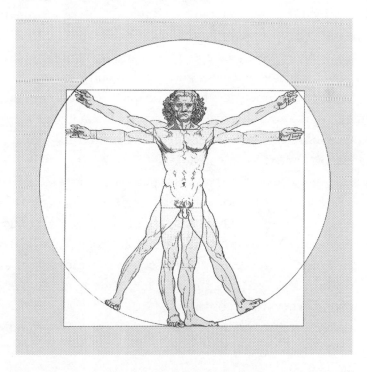

Figure 3: The Vitruvian Man

"You feel clean and pure. When I visited the Western countries, I saw some drawings of this sphere. People call it the '*Leonardo Sphere*', because of the drawings of Leonardo da Vinci; in fact, this illustration of the human body, which is inscribed in the circle and the square, derives from a passage on geometry and the human proportions in the writings of Vitruvius. It had been created almost 1,600 years before Leonardo da Vinci," said Karma Dorje.

Basically, the reason why average people lack energy and will, is that they have never cleaned their lives and their lives are full of heavily loaded emotions, memories, fears, and so on," Tenzin Dhargey explained.

"Do you mean that we have to clean our energies from the past?" I asked in surprise.

"That is correct, dear Tenzin Rinchen. That is correct" replied Tenzin Dhargey with a smile.

"Cleaning our energies from the past and high consciousness go hand-in-hand. The more you clean, you release the energy that has been imprisoned within you from others and without this liberation of energy you cannot reach a higher level of consciousness.

"Cleaning our energies from the past is not the same as remembering. Remembering is a normal day-to-day type of thinking, while cleaning our energies from the past is done through conscious movement of the energy.

"Cleaning our energies from the past is the key to shifting to a higher consciousness. So, you must begin by cleaning the large incidents first. By merely thinking about them you actually have to shift yourself to the place where the event took place. When you do that -when you are at the place of the event- move your energy exactly to how it was at the time of the incident, when the event took place," Karma Dorje continued.

"Do you mean that I have to '*see*' the incident as if I am watching it in a movie?" I asked puzzled.

"Cleaning our energies from the past means to recollect and clean life events down to the smallest detail. I will tell you how it works and you can start doing it right now," Tenzin Dhargey replied.

"There are two stages of '***Cleaning Energies from the Past***':

"**First Stage**: a brief account of all the incidents in our lives that stand out for examination in an obvious manner;

"**Second Stage**: a more detailed recollection of the incidents. This systematically starts at a point right in the moment before the cleaning phase and it theoretically extends to the moment of birth or to the period during time you were in your mother's womb.

"You must understand that cleaning our lives never ends, no matter how well we have done it once.

"Sometimes it helps to make a list of all the people we have met in our life starting from the present. You will find that you have had an issue with half the people you have met, a thought about that person or an interaction with that person.

"The key element of the *'Cleaning our Energies from the Past'* meditation is breathing. Breathing helps reach deeper and deeper memories."

Cleaning Energies from the Past Meditation:

- ❖ Write down a list of incidents.
- ❖ Sit in a comfortable posture with your spine straight and hands facing each other; palms relaxed on the knees or at the level of your heart (it might be more comfortable to place them on your knees).
- ❖ Move into your Heart.
- ❖ *Initial Breath*: Inhale deeply and slowly and, at the same time, bring your hands together, facing each other and without touching. Exhale long and slowly and bring the hands back to the initial position, placed on the knees and facing each other.
- ❖ Take the first incident from the top of your list and remain with it until all the feelings spent in it have been reviewed. Reconstruct the event, piece by piece, starting by recollecting

the physical details of the surroundings, then going to the person whom you shared the interaction with and then turning to yourself to examine your feelings.

❖ As you remember, a feeling will arise in the event. Inhale deeply and slowly and, at the same time, bring your hands together, facing each other and without touching. The function of this breathing is to restore energy. This is how you pick up the energy that has been left behind.

❖ Exhale long and slowly and bring the hands back to the initial position, placed on the knees and facing each other. By exhaling, the energy that had been left in you by other people who were involved in the event that you are recollecting, will be ejected.

❖ Forgive yourself and the person involved in the incident.

"Retrieving your energy that has been left in the world, and rejecting the energy that others have left in you, cleans your energy and brings a higher vibration in you, which allows you to proceed further in life, detached and unbiased.

"It might take more than a meditation to clean an incident; you might need to do it again and again until you feel good about the incident and when you recall it your energy is unbiased by the issue. You are completely detached by it." Karma Dorje explained.

CHAPTER 11

Cleaning the Energy of our Day

I am very impressed by the 'Cleaning Energies from the Past' meditation. It is very powerful. Yesterday I spent all day doing it. I really feel that my energy is cleaner now," I said to the Masters, enchanted by the results of the meditation.

"This meditation is very important. The thing is that it does not just take a day to clean your past; sometimes it takes lives to clean all your karmic issues," Karma Dorje replied.

"There are two important meditations that help clean your past: The 'Cleaning Energies from the Past' meditation helps clean past incidents and the 'Cleaning Energy of Your Day' exercise helps clean your day that has just ended," Karma Dorje continued.

"Yes, actually I was thinking how we could clean our 'short-term' accumulated energies. So, *there is* a method to clean the day that has just ended?" I asked the Masters.

"Yes, there is; it is a method that is very easy to do. You just need to persevere and keep doing it without stopping it. Each night, before you fall asleep and just when you are ready to fall asleep, mentally go through the activities of the whole day, backwards.

"This is a remembering process.

"Start from the moment you got into bed -which is the last activity- and go backwards, step by step, to the first activity of that morning when you first awoke.

"Remember the day - anything that has happened. Look at it, but do not get involved in it. It is like watching a movie; you see a form there, but it is not you. You are just a witness, attentive and aware of the activity.

"You are just an observer; you do not judge anything that has happened during the day. If you had an argument with a friend, it is the form that is arguing now, not you. Watch the whole thing as if somebody else is there, not you. Do not get involved; do not get angry again. If you get angry again, you have identified with the form. Look at your past in a detached manner, dis-identified.

"This exercise has been widely used by all Masters, especially by Buddha and Mahavira. Buddha taught his disciples that this method helps become formless; like water that flows and changes continuously.

"The secret is to do it backwards and to be detached."

Let us review the steps in 'Cleaning the Energy of our Day' exercise.

❖ Turn off the lights, lie down, close your eyes and totally relax.

❖ When you feel either very heavy or so light that you are almost floating, begin looking at your day backwards. It will be as if you are watching a movie; see a form there, but it is not you. You are just a witness, attentive and aware of each activity.

❖ Move back through your day's activities; watch everything as if it is somebody else there, not you. Do not get involved; do not get angry or happy again. Do not get upset or elated.

❖ Start from the moment you got into bed -which is the last activity- and go backwards, step by step, to the first activity in the morning when you first awoke.

❖ "The 'Cleaning Energies from the Past' meditation and the 'Cleaning the Energy of our Day' exercise are essential tools for liberation and enlightenment.

❖ "If you do the 'Cleaning Energies from the Past' meditation from time to time and the 'Cleaning the Energy of our Day' exercise each night before falling asleep, then your level of consciousness will rise and you will become enlightened very soon," Karma Dorje explained.

CHAPTER 12

The School of the Heart

I am thinking of gathering all this information I am receiving here and when I return I will begin a spiritual team called '*The School of the Heart*'. Do you believe that would be a good idea?" I asked the Masters one day.

"This is your call, dear Tenzin. This is your call," replied Tenzin Dhargey with a smile.

"All spiritual organizations of this world are trying to work with the polarities we live in. However, instead of creating love, almost all create hate and frustration. The reason is because we live in a world of polarities.

"We are used to possessing things. The leaders of these organizations or the team that continues the leader's work when the leader is not there anymore, sooner or later becomes corrupted and greatly deviates from the initial spiritual manifest.

"What was in the beginning a nice dream, later becomes a nightmare. So it is your call," repeated Karma Dorje.

I was surprised by the Masters' assessment and asked: "Why does this happen? Are not these organizations supposed to be leading us to God?"

"Do we need somebody to lead us to God? We have the free-will to go to God without any 'leaders'. We can do it without churches, or temples or anything else.

"But, since we live our lives like robots, we need leaders. We need somebody to create the future for us. But what people must understand is that the future is created by the past. Because we live like robots, we become very predictable. Our future is possible because the past repeats itself.

"Jesus or Buddha did not need to follow any organization. They lived here and now. They were unpredictable. They understood that reality is here, now.

"We live like machines, continuously running and while we are running, we see our lives pass by without understanding anything. Basically, we project our future based on our past.

"The only thing you can teach in your School of the Heart is that life is all there is, dear Tenzin. The only thing you can teach in your School of the Heart is that people must live fully and intensely. If you can teach them that, then your School of the Heart makes sense," Karma Dorje continued.

"So, basically, we must fully make the most of the present, because it is not going to come back to us, is it?" I asked the Masters.

"That is true. There should be a reason you call it the School of the Heart, instead of School of the Mind.

"The mind is just a sum of thoughts. These thoughts become words, because we are not able to stay in silence too much. So, we are just words, empty words. But the heart is beyond words. We think we are the mind and, if you are not aware of your mind, then nothing good comes to you.

"But when we identify ourselves with our mind, in fact we identify ourselves with something that is not alive, but a shadow.

"So you need to teach people to be centered in their hearts. This is the first thing you need to do. And this is the most important spiritual technique.

"So, create your School of the Heart if you feel people need this spiritual work," Tenzin Dhargey encouraged.

*   *   *

I remembered the story of the twelve Imagery Master Children that had met in 1991 near Jerusalem who had written on a stone: "If it is not simple, simple it is not going to be".

PART FOUR

Heart Imagery

To you, my beloved reader.
Remember that this book did not come into your hands by chance.
Your Higher Self gave it to you for a reason:
to remember who you really are!

CHAPTER 13

History of Heart Imagery

oday we will approach a very important subject. If you comprehend just a fraction of this, then your level of consciousness will be on the highest level of achievement! It regards Heart Imagery - *Snying Gnasjal*," said Karma Dorje with an enigmatic smile.

"Yes, I vaguely remember that we spoke about it long time ago," I remarked, puzzled by the Master's statement.

"We are going to start a set of exercises that will continue, more or less, for a full month. By 'we', I refer to Tenzin, myself and your Higher Self. Some of the exercises will come from yourself; from your Higher Self. Later, you will remember some of the most important exercises and you will help others who are still sleeping to start their awakening process.

"Remember when we met that I told you that now you are asleep? You were always asleep. Actually, we are all dreaming; night and day; continuously," said Karma Dorje.

"Are these exercises part of Tibetan meditation tradition?" I asked curiously.

"Nothing of what we are teaching you is part of the Tibetan tradition!" Karma Dorje replied.

I definitely looked stupefied, as both Masters started laughing.

"Who do you think we are?" Tenzin Dhargey looked into my eyes and asked.

"Tibetan Masters!" I mumbled completely puzzled by their question.

"Why Tibetan? Why do you call it 'Tibetan tradition'? Do you believe that the place you were born is related with the level of your consciousness? Do you not believe that all Masters of this world share the same teachings? Do not all of us teach the same thing?" Karma Dorje asked me.

"I guess you do..." I answered.

"These exercises are older than Tibet itself, my dear Tenzin! When the Material Son and Daughter of God, whom we call here Adam and Eve, came to upgrade our DNA and our consciousness, the people who had remained after they had gone, started using Heart Imagery techniques. Heart Imagery was used primarily by the Violet Race or the Adamic Race and later by the Vedics and the Sumerians.

"The first descendants of Adam and Eve, the Adamic Race or the Adamsonites, preserved the Heart Imagery exercises and continued to use them for over seven thousand years.

"The centre of their civilization was near Kopet Dag, near the Caspian Sea, in Turkmenistan, close to Iran. There in the highlands of Kopet Dag, were the headquarters of the Adamic or Violet Race.

"Four different groups of the Adamic Race migrated from Kopet Dag: the first group went to the Americas, the second group migrated to Greece, to the Mediterranean Islands and the Middle East area; the third group went to India and Tibet, where they formed the Andite-Aryans. The fourth group went to Europe.

"The Andites had tried to preserve the Heart Imagery spiritual work for over fifteen thousand years in the basin of the Tarim River in Sinkiang and in the South in the highland regions of Tibet, where the Andites had moved to from the Mesopotamia area. The Tarim Valley had been the centre of the true Andite culture. They built their settlements there and entered into trade relations with the progressive Chinese in the East and with the Andonites in the North. Their spiritual systems took over whatever remained of these powerful imagery techniques and they used them to balance their energies and understand higher dimensions," Tenzin Dhargey explained.

I was really surprised by this history lesson given to me by Tenzin Dhargey and Karma Dorje.

"How do you know all these details?" I asked curiously.

"We were there." Karma Dorje replied very matter-of-factly.

Intuitively I knew that my Masters could do things that lied beyond my comprehension.

I suddenly felt that, in fact, they were part of the group of Adamic Masters; I knew that they were more than human.

"The exercises are very simple and efficient. The order of the exercises, in the manner they were given to us, is not by chance. Each set of exercises is related with your subtle energy and it moves it towards the right direction. The secret of these exercises, from the teacher's point of view, is to know when the human mind kicks in and starts chatting; when the logical part of the brain, the left side, starts interfering. As a teacher of these techniques you must be aware of this before it happens, in order to give the next exercise!" Tenzin Dhargey explained.

"We will work on exercises from the Heart Imagery system, night and day for the period of one month, continuously until you completely quieten your mind and remember who you really are. Years from now, you might be able to remember the most powerful exercises that influenced your energy, and you might want to share your knowledge with other people.

"You will understand that life and death are interrelated and that everything around us is just an image. You will understand that death helps you see beyond this life and see other dimensions. You will become aware of death so deeply that the future will become your present. You will see death and life as part of the Universe's creation," concluded Tenzin Dhargey as he smiled at me.

"Before beginning the exercises, you will need to clean your main chakras again. We will use a soft chanting and some ancient mantras that will clean the energy of your chakras. You will also see colors, images, lights and other expressions of the main five chakras that your senses will be able to perceive," said Karma Dorje.

"We call this meditation the '*Divine Chanting Meditation*' and we usually have some young monks chant in a very soft tone in the background.

"When you go back into the world, you can use some soft meditation music that resonates with your heart."

Steps for the Divine Chanting Meditation:

Move into the Heart.

Place your attention on the first chakra at the base of your body, at your perineum. See a beautiful red color; the mantra word for this chakra is LAM. Chant the mantra LAM gently from your heart, until you feel it spreading throughout your body.

Place your attention on the second chakra behind your navel and see a shining orange-yellow color; the mantra word for this chakra is VAM. Chant the mantra VAM gently from your heart, until you feel it spreading throughout your body.

Place your attention on the third chakra behind the middle of your chest and see a nourishing green color like the grass in springtime; the mantra word for this chakra is YAM. Chant the mantra YAM gently from your heart, until you feel it spreading throughout your body.

Place your attention on the fourth chakra in the middle of your forehead and see a deep dark blue or indigo color, like the night sky on a summer night. This is where the third eye or the seat of your dreams and visions is. The mantra word for this chakra is SHAM; chant the mantra SHAM gently from your heart, until you feel it spreading throughout your body.

Place your attention on the fifth chakra on the top of your head and see a shining gold-white glowing light; this is the crown chakra or the seat of Divinity; the mantra word for this chakra is AUM. Chant the mantra AUM gently from your heart, until you feel it spreading throughout your body.

I started practicing this meditation and I felt an instant relief of unsettled energies within my chakras. I felt how the vibration of my chanting was really cleaning all my bodies: the physical, the mental and the emotional body. While I changed the mantras, the Masters were softly chanting the same words in divine union of their magnificent voices. I was always delighted by their soft and, at the same time, powerful voices when they chanted. Their voices would emanate a strange combination of alpha and theta waves that automatically put me into a meditation state.

*   *   *

"Could you tell me more about Heart Imagery? It seems such a simple, yet powerful spiritual system," I asked the Masters.

"Heart Imagery is an ancient spiritual system coming from the ancient times. The Tibetan, Sumerian and Vedic spiritual mystery schools have been using it for thousands of years. It is related with the highest number of Mystery Schools: 555. We will also talk about Sacred Numerology later on," said Tenzin Dhargey.

"Heart Imagery helps and teaches you to balance your mental, emotional and physical bodies and it harmonizes your energy. In the future, especially after December 21, 2012 when Mother Earth will change her energy from masculine to feminine, Heart Imagery will be the most important technique that one could do, in order to bring harmony inside and outside!

"Heart Imagery exercises offer a pure experience: they are a set of key exercises that open your possibilities to see, sense and feel other dimensions.

"Unlike other spiritual systems, Heart Imagery exercises create freedom from the illusions of ego created by the mind.

"It is that part, from your heart, that helps you become a Master; to develop the awareness within that brings light and love. Right now the master in your heart is asleep. And the mind, the servant, is playing the role of the master. And the servant is not even your servant; the servant is created by the outside world, it follows the outside world and its laws.

"Once you enlighten your awareness through Heart Imagery exercises, it burns up the whole slavery that the mind has created. You will become a Master of your own destiny.

"In Heart Imagery you learn to surrender yourself; to allow your ego to disappear. It is a set of "minor surrenders" that prepare you for the major, the total surrender when you lose your ego and the flowing light and energy comes to you!" said Karma Dorje.

"Mastering heart imagery techniques will open to you to the possibility of seeing the light of the heart and feel the sound or the inner vibration," concluded Tenzin Dhargey looking at me to see if I could comprehend the importance of what they told me.

I presume that I had a very serious and solemn face as both Great Masters started laughing.

"Above all, remember that this is just a dream, dear Tenzin. Do not try to analyze everything you see or sense. Just let it be. Just let the effect of the image work inside you. Just smile and feel free, dear Tenzin. You will soon understand that you are formless within a form," Tenzin Dhargey advised.

CHAPTER 14

Cleaning the Past & Self-Renewal

During the month that followed, I could not honestly tell whether I was in a dream or in what we call 'reality'.

The images that the Masters or my Higher Self were giving me where so real that I had to ask myself a couple of times whether I was still there with them or if I had transported inside of that image. I understood why the Masters told me that I would feel the inner sound and see the inner light.

I had found the sound of silence. Somewhere between or during the exercises, I felt the sound of soundlessness and saw glimpses of divine light. I had lost all my fears. I realized that, during these exercises, I had the same feeling that I used to experience when I was just two or three years old and my mum would play with me. I was not afraid. I was a child playing with his mother; I had opened up and become vulnerable; detached and without any worries. I was like a child again: innocent, pure, eternal and the universe was my home.

It is difficult to split or break the Heart Imagery techniques into categories, but I could say that there were three clear trends developing in the exercises given by the Masters.

The first one regards cleaning the past. There was a clear tendency towards this direction during the first week.

Then, we spent almost two weeks healing the body, the organs inside the body and emotional traumas.

And finally, during the last week, I was given exercises that purified my mind, my heart, my spirit and my soul. The purpose of these sets of exercises and meditations where to connect with divinity and achieve union with God.

Each time we had a group of exercises that we would do together; Tenzin Dhargey or Karma Dorje would give the exercise, but I could feel that both Masters were also practicing it. After that, we would have a practical exercise each evening that I would have to do alone, to practice for a couple of hours until the Masters came back and we would resume the practice with a new set of exercises and meditations.

Obviously, it is almost impossible for me to write down all the exercises that we did together with the Masters, but I will write at least some of the most important exercises and meditations that we did together. I will try my best to give clear explanations and descriptions for all three categories:

> **Heart Imagery** - Cleaning the Past and Self-Renewal
> **Heart Imagery** - Healing and Emotional Clarity
> **Heart Imagery** - Union with God

* * *

The first set of exercises (*Cleaning the Past and Self-Renewal*) helped me understand the Heart Imagery Mystery School and it helped me clean my past and rebirth myself.

We all carry unclean energy from the past. There is a lot of imprisoned energy within us that has been left over from others. If we do not release this energy, we will not be able to understand and move to a higher level of consciousness.

Some suggestions for this imagery:

Close your eyes (it would be a good idea to use a sleeping mask), sit upright in a chair or in a half lotus posture (be comfortable). Breathe-in 3 times through your nostrils and breathe out through your mouth; your hands should be open and the palms facing down.

In heart imagery, the shorter time you stay with an image, the more powerful the result will be. A Master in Imagery knows when the brain of the student is ready to kick-in and that is the moment when he gives another image that keeps the student in the heart and the brain quiet.

Be a child again; do not analyze what you see, sense or feel. Let it happen naturally.

If you wish to practice the exercises, you will need somebody else to read them to you; it is not advised to read them or learn them off by heart, because that is when your mind will take over. The exercises are actually designed actually to quieten your mind, your brain. It will not, therefore, work if you read them and practice them. Trying to remember them involves the left brain, the logical and mental body.

But even when somebody else reads the exercises to you, that person must feel when the logical side of your brain, when your mental body, has begun to take over.

I know for sure that, whenever the Masters gave me an exercise, they knew exactly when my mind kicked in. I felt they would open their third eye and "see" me when I stopped using the imagery system.

They knew when to give me the next exercise.

The first exercise is to always move our spirit from the brain to the heart.

Heart Imagery Exercise: Moving from the Brain to the Heart
- ❖ Close your eyes.
- ❖ Relax and begin to breathe rhythmically.
- ❖ Perform a long, slow exhalation through your mouth, followed by a normal inhalation through the nose. Do this three times and once you have exhaled, see and feel that all your thoughts, concerns, worries, issues, problems, any sickness or pain have gone and that you are in harmony and love

❖ See, sense and feel that a set of stairs is leading from your brain down to your heart and that you have started moving down these stairs.

❖ Stop right in front of your heart where you find a door. Open it and remember to close the door behind you.

❖ Step in and look around you and see, sense and feel the space of your Heart

❖ Inhale the sweet energy of the heart; feel the peace and harmony of the heart. Feel the unconditional love energy from your heart.

Heart Imagery Exercise: Cleaning the Past and Self-Renewal

Remember that if you want to practice these exercises, you need somebody else to read them to you; reading them or learning them off by heart will cause your mind to take over and you will lose all the positive effects of this exercise.

Blue Cloud Exercise

❖ Move to the Heart (use the Exercise: Moving from the Brain to the Heart mentioned above)

❖ Breathe out once (breathe out a long, slow exhalation through your mouth. Do this once).

❖ See, sense and feel that you are an empty vessel. See, sense and feel that a blue cloud comes and it enters your body from the top of your head (as if you have an opening there): a pure blue light is inside of you now.

❖ See how the blue colored cloud goes out of your body through your toes and fingers: in the beginning the color is not very pure, but after a few seconds it becomes clear and it is like the pure blue sky.

❖ Continue receiving the blue cloud inside you from the top of your head until you see, sense and feel that the color of the cloud that is going out of your body through your fingers and toes is exactly the same color as the cloud that had entered from the top of your head.

❖ Breathe out once.

❖ See, sense and feel that you are completely clean, inside and out, and that you are connected with the whole universe.

❖ Breathe out once and open your eyes.

❖ Write down your experience.

Ocean Water Exercise

❖ Move to the Heart.

❖ Breathe out once (breathe out a long, slow exhalation through your mouth. Do this once).

❖ See, sense and feel that you are an empty vessel with an opening at the top.

❖ See, sense and feel that you are floating over the pure, clean blue transparent water of the ocean.

❖ Now go into the water. Feel the water is enter your body and clean you; see, sense and feel all you have inside is clean, pure water.

❖ Breathe out once.

❖ See, sense and feel that you and the water have become one; there is only water mass and the ocean and yourself are one.

❖ Breathe out once and open your eyes.

❖ Write down your experience.

Mountain Rock Exercise

❖ Move to the Heart.

❖ Breathe out once (breathe out a long, slow exhalation through your mouth. Do this once).

❖ See, sense and feel that you are walking on a mountain trail.

❖ See that in front of you, right in the middle of the trail, is a big, giant rock.

❖ See, sense, feel and know that you can go through the rock; feel that you are walking through it.

❖ Breathe out once.

❖ See, sense and feel that you are leaving behind all your issues and problems inside the rock (one minute).

❖ See, sense and feel that, soon, you will have finished passing through the rock.

❖ You only have ten steps left to go: 10, 9, 8, 7, 6, 5, 4, 3, 2, 1.

❖ You have passed through the rock now.

❖ Breathe out once.

❖ What is the difference between entering the rock and after having passed through it?

❖ Breathe out once and open your eyes.

❖ Write down your experience.

Schools Colleagues and Friends Cleaning Exercise

❖ Move to the Heart.

❖ Breathe out once (breathe out a long, slow exhalation through your mouth. Do this once).

❖ See, sense and feel that you are a little child with your childhood friends. If there is something to clean there, go ahead and clean it. If there are some children or friends who have trespassed or hurt you, forgive them. If you have hurt somebody, forgive yourself. Try to feel their energy from your perspective now. How do you feel?

❖ Breathe out once.

❖ See, sense and feel that you are in high school amongst your classmates. If there is something to clean there, go ahead and clean it. If there are some colleagues who have trespassed or hurt you, forgive them. If you have hurt anyone, forgive yourself. See, sense and feel their energy from your perspective now. Without judging, just feel their energy. How do you feel?

❖ Breathe out once.

❖ See, sense and feel that you are at University with your friends and course mates. If there is something to clean there, go ahead and clean it. Feel their energy.

❖ Breathe out once.

❖ See, sense and feel that you are with your friends and colleagues now. If there is something to clean there, go ahead and clean it. How do you feel and see their energy now?

❖ See, sense and feel that you are with your friends and colleagues in the future. If there is something to clean there, go ahead and clean it. How do you feel and see their energy now?

❖ See, sense and feel that you are one: the past, the present and the future are the same. The little child, the teenager, the adult and the future adult you will become, are all the same. How do you feel now?

❖ Breathe out once and open your eyes.

❖ Write down your experience.

Cleaning the Room of the Mind exercise

❖ Move to the Heart.

❖ Breathe out once (breathe out a long, slow exhalation through your mouth. Do this once).

❖ See, sense and feel that you are in a big, big room with hundreds of different sized boxes, similar to those in a warehouse. Each box represents one of your thoughts.

❖ Breathe out once.

❖ Look in front of you and realize that the room is infinite, it has no end; you cannot see the end.

❖ Breathe out once.

❖ See, sense and feel that on your left hand side is a big, giant hole, like a vacuum.

❖ With your intention, start the vacuum cleaner and see the boxes disappearing one by one into the hole. The vacuum increases the speed and nearly all the boxes have gone now.

❖ See, sense and feel now that the room is empty. How do you feel? Analyze how it feels to be empty, without thoughts.

❖ Breathe out once and open your eyes.

❖ Write down your experience.

Cleaning Mother Earth Exercise

- ❖ Move to the Heart.
- ❖ Breathe out once (breathe out a long, slow exhalation through your mouth. Do this once).
- ❖ See, sense and feel you are a cleaner of Mother Earth.
- ❖ See, sense and feel that you have become enormous and that Mother Earth is in your hands.
- ❖ Breathe out once.
- ❖ See, sense and feel that you are on another planet and you have Mother Earth in your hands. Place her under beautiful, spring water.
- ❖ Clean all the dirt off Mother Earth. See the brown water coming off, until it becomes clean and until you see the beautiful oceans and mountains.
- ❖ Breathe out once.
- ❖ Take Mother Earth and put her back.
- ❖ Breathe out once.
- ❖ See, sense and feel now that you are on a clean planet. How do you feel?
- ❖ Breathe out once and open your eyes.
- ❖ Write down your experience.

Air-Body exercise

- ❖ Move to the Heart.
- ❖ Breathe out once (breathe out a long, slow exhalation through your mouth. Do this once).
- ❖ See, sense and feel that you are dissolving into pure air.
- ❖ See, sense and feel that you are in the lungs of all people and animals.
- ❖ See, sense and feel that you are in plants; all over the planet.
- ❖ Now feel that the air has become dense and you and all the air particles get together and structure your body again.
- ❖ What is the difference between before, when you were just air, and now that you are a body?

❖ Breathe out once and open your eyes.
❖ Write down your experience.

Gazing exercise

❖ Move to the Heart.
❖ Breathe out once (breathe out a long, slow exhalation through your mouth. Do this once).
❖ See, sense and feel that you are in a beautiful meadow amongst trees and that you are sitting in a lotus posture, gazing at a crystal that is right in the middle of the meadow.
❖ See, sense and feel that the crystal is alive and ready to take over all your past issues, problems, worries and resentments.
❖ See, sense and feel that a river of light is standing between you and the crystal and, all your past issues, problems, worries and resentments, are moving and flowing from you to the crystal.
❖ See, sense and feel that the crystal is transmuting all negative energies, they have left you and they have changed into positive energies.
❖ See, sense and feel that the energies are coming back to you through the river of light and that you did not lose any energy.
❖ What is the difference between gazing at the crystal and now that you have you connected with it?
❖ Breathe out once and open your eyes.
❖ Write down your experience.

Waterfall exercise

❖ Move to the Heart.
❖ Breathe out once (breathe out a long, slow exhalation through your mouth. Do this once).
❖ See, sense and feel that you are an empty vessel under a waterfall that is cleaning all the impurities of your physical body; the pure water enters your body and cleans all your organs.

❖ Breathe out once.

❖ See, sense and feel that you are an empty vessel under a waterfall of light that is cleaning the energy inside and out of your body.

❖ Breathe out once.

❖ What is the difference between going under the waterfall and now that you have come out of the waterfall?

❖ Breathe out once and open your eyes.

❖ Write down your experience.

The Desert Exercise

❖ Move to the Heart.

❖ Breathe out once (breathe out a long, slow exhalation through your mouth. Do this once).

❖ See, sense and feel that you are in the middle of the desert; you are sitting in a lotus posture.

❖ Feel the wind. Feel transparent. The sand is sifting through you and it is cleaning you. It is coming from the left, rotating around your emotional body and then it is going to your right, taking all your particles with it.

❖ See, sense and feel how the sand is changing color as it sifts through you, from yellow on your left side, to brownish after it has passed through you towards the right.

❖ Breathe out once and open your eyes.

❖ Write down your experience.

The Planet Keeper Exercise

❖ Move to the Heart.

❖ Breathe out once (breathe out a long, slow exhalation through your mouth. Do this once).

❖ See, sense and feel that you are the keeper of all animals on this planet. You are the one who takes care of all the animals on this planet. Elephants, lions, fish, whales, dolphins. You are like a zookeeper, but there is no zoo, just Mother Earth. How do you feel?

❖ Breathe out once.
❖ See, sense and feel now that you are taking care of all plants, flowers and trees on this planet. How do you feel now?
❖ Breathe out once.
❖ See, sense and feel that you are the keeper of all landscapes; water, mountains, desert, continents, all stones, crystals. You are the keeper of all these forms. How do you feel?
❖ Breathe out once and open your eyes.
❖ Write down your experience.

The Timekeeper of the Universe

❖ Move to the Heart.
❖ Breathe out once (breathe out a long, slow exhalation through your mouth. Do this once).
❖ See, sense and feel and know that you are walking on an infinite road. Just keep walking. How do you feel walking on this infinite road that has no end and no beginning? Whatever you experience is welcome.
❖ Breathe out once.
❖ See, sense and feel as if you are jumping from one planet to another. Jump from Earth to Mars, from Mars to Pluto, from Pluto to Jupiter, and then onto other planets. Feel this energy, as you are jumping from one planet to another, as you travel through the Universe. How do you feel?
❖ Breathe out once.
❖ See, sense and feel that you are the timekeeper of the Universe. In your left hand you are holding time, you have places where there is time. In your right hand, you have places where there is no time. How do you feel being the timekeeper? Do you feel balanced? Do you feel the energy? Left hand: time. Right hand: no time.
❖ Breathe out once and open your eyes.
❖ Write down your experience.

The Body as a Flower Exercise

❖ Move to the Heart.

❖ Breathe out once (breathe out a long, slow exhalation through your mouth. Do this once).

❖ See, sense and feel that your body is a flower bud; your head is the bud of the flower. What do you experience?

❖ Now see, sense and feel in your body events, emotions and situations from your life. How does the flower react to this? For some events you might feel that the flower almost dries up and for some events the flower glows in light and emanates a pleasant fragrance.

❖ Breathe out once.

❖ See, sense and feel that all humanity has become like what you are now: flower buds. And that the whole humanity senses its events and emotions as you are doing now.

❖ Feel that, after we get over all our emotions, then all of us, all the flowers, are glowing in light and we are like a planet with nice, beautiful, flowers

❖ Breathe out once and open your eyes.

❖ Write down your experience.

The House Exercise

❖ Move to the Heart.

❖ Breathe out once (breathe out a long, slow exhalation through your mouth. Do this once).

❖ See, sense and feel that you are in front of a house and you know that inside the house you have manifested all past angers, frustrations and resentments. Go inside of the house and start cleaning it. Take a broom and clean the floor, take the dust, paint the walls in your favorite colors.

❖ Breathe out once.

❖ Now go outside and clean the garden and turn the exterior of the house into the way you would like it to be.

❖ Go inside the house again, bring a comfortable chair near the window and sit there looking outside. How do you feel now that you have cleaned the house?

❖ Breathe out once and open your eyes.

❖ Write down your experience.

*   *   *

Practical exercises that can be used in our daily activities without meditation.

"Switch" your Energy Exercise

This exercise is to be done first with a Heart Imagery Teacher, in order to understand how to switch the energy.

When you get into a reaction, into a secondary instinct, try to recognize the emotion which the basic energy has transformed into and has now become a secondary instinct. For example: you may have become depressed (*emotion*) and have gone to sleep upset and angry (*secondary instinct*).

When you feel that the energy is changing into an emotion (*depression*), as soon as you feel the first signs of the emotion in you, switch your energy to harmony: see the word 'HARMONY' written with golden letters in front of you and visualize that you are in harmony.

What image do you have for being in harmony? Maybe you see that you are in sitting a lotus posture in meditation or that you are sitting quietly in a park quietly, enjoying nature or up in the mountains, in the middle of a forest of cedar trees with a spring water nearby.

Breathe out once.

CHAKRAS, INSTINCTS, ORGANS and FEELINGS

SECONDARY INSTINCTS	EMOTIONS	PRIMARY INSTINCTS	CHAKRAS	ORGANS	FEELINGS RESPONSES
Fight	Fury Irritation	Survival	Crown	Brain Fontanel	Peace Clarity
Sleeping Disorders	Depression	Sight Sleep	Third Eye	Brain Pineal Gland Thyroid Gland	Harmony
Quiet or uncontrollable talking	Anxiety	Speech	Throat	Thyroid Gland	Turst Balance
Breathing very fast Smoking	Hate Resentment	Breathing	Heart	Heart Lungs Thymus Gland	Love Joy Compassion
Eating Disorders Alcohol Addiction	Frustration	Nourishment	Will Power	Kidneys Adrenal Gland	Calmness
Sexual Disorders	Anxiety	Reproduction	Sex	Genitals Reproductive Glands	Creativity
Becoming Afraid Insecurity	Fear	Movement	Base	Perineum	Courage

Water exercise

Pour water into a glass and keep the glass in your hands for 10 seconds while focusing all your attention on the water.

With your intention, send light and love to the water from your heart through your hands directly to the water and say to the water 3 times: "I love you".

See, sense and feel that the water has become structured and alive.

Drink the water slowly and, as you swallow it down, say to the water 3 times: "I love you, I love you, I love you".

Stop and breathe exercise

Remember to STOP 3 times a day from whatever you are doing (computer, work, shopping, watching TV) just for 10 seconds and remember to breathe: take 3 long inhalations through your nostrils and 3 long exhalations through your mouth.

We have habits and we need to pause from them. We need to make some time to return to our bodies each day.

Clean the Dreams Exercise

Remember that whatever you dream of, is your truth; it has been created by yourself. Do not blame somebody else for your dreams, because you are the one who has created them.

How to clean your nightmares or the dreams that make you feel uncomfortable:

The first step is to understand your dreams. You cannot understand a dream while you are sleeping, because you are in the dream.

So first program yourself prior to fall asleep to remember the dream.

In the morning when you wake up, take each dream and meditate. Do not be afraid. Go back in the dream. Remember that fear is there to teach you courage.

Clean the dream: if you have dreamt a house that is dirty and messy, then clean the house, clean it all; clean the dream until you feel happy, calm, relaxed.

Unnecessary Repetitions

Unnecessary Repetitions are a big alarm for your energy. Check yourself. Whenever you do one of these unnecessary repetitions you lose energy.

Do you perhaps have bell-words, such as "whatever" or any other words? Do you have tics, like twirling your hair or scratching your head when somebody asks you a difficult question? Find them all and be aware when you tend to do each one.

At the beginning you will be caught by the habit of saying it or doing it, but in time you will do it less and less.

When you stop all the unnecessary repetitions you will not be tired anymore. Instead, you will feel fresh and you will have enough energy to get through the day.

CHAPTER 15

Healing & Emotional Clarity

Remember that if you want to practice these exercises, you need somebody else to read it to you; reading them or remembering them off by heart will cause your mind to take over and you will lose all the positive effects of this exercise.

The Sun Exercise
- ❖ Move to the Heart.
- ❖ Breathe out once (breathe out a long, slow exhalation through your mouth. Do this once).
- ❖ See yourself sitting outside in a garden or in a park in the morning at time of the day when the sun is up at the level of your forehead.
- ❖ See, sense and feel that the warm and the light of the Sun have reached you.
- ❖ See, sense and feel the Sun coming slowly, slowly to your head, your forehead. The Sun is entering right through the middle of your forehead and it is now inside your head.
- ❖ Turn your eyes inwards and see the Sun inside of your head.
- ❖ Breathe out once.
- ❖ See the Sun coming slowly down through your throat, powerfully lightening up your throat.
- ❖ See the Sun coming slowly down and inside your upper chest area, shining powerfully in that whole area.
- ❖ See the Sun coming slowly down to your lower chest area, warming it all up.
- ❖ See the Sun coming slowly down to your stomach area.
- ❖ See the Sun coming slowly down to your abdomen area, warming up it all up.

❖ Breathe out once.

❖ See, sense and feel that the warmth and the light of the Sun are going inside your kidneys and from there up through your spine. The spine is like a tree and the light is going around the spine from left to right, exactly like the branches of a tree.

❖ Breathe out once and open your eyes.

❖ Write down your experience.

The Moon Exercise

❖ Move to the Heart.

❖ Breathe out once (breathe out a long, slow exhalation through your mouth. Do this once).

❖ See yourself sitting outside in a garden or in a park in the evening when the Moon is up shining on a beautiful night sky.

❖ See, sense and feel that the white light of the Moon is coming to you.

❖ See, sense and feel that the Moon is coming slowly, slowly down to your feet, in front of you. The Moon is entering right through the soles of your feet.

❖ See, sense and feel that the white, clear light of the Moon is cleaning out your right foot and your left foot.

❖ See, sense and feel that the light of the Moon is going up, cleaning your right knee and your left knee.

❖ See, sense and feel that the white light of the Moon is going up, cleaning your right hip and your left hip.

❖ Breathe out once.

❖ See, sense and feel that the sparkling white light of the Moon is going up from your hips to your spine, all over your body and your organs. The spine is like a tree and the light is going around the spine from left to right, exactly like the branches of a tree.

❖ Breathe out once and open your eyes.

❖ Write down your experience.

The Lake Exercise

- ❖ Move to the Heart.
- ❖ See, sense and feel that you are floating on a lake on a beautiful night, facing up towards a clear sky, and that you see thousands of stars.
- ❖ See, sense and feel that the sky is mirrored in the lake and seven stars are mirrored directly onto your chakras.
- ❖ See how your seven chakras are shining and are cleaned by the seven stars.
- ❖ Now see that you are moving up to the sky and the real stars are mirrored in your transparent body; see the lake and the stars down onto the lake; feel that you are in both places now: on the lake and in the sky.
- ❖ Gently let yourself move back from the sky and connect with your physical body.
- ❖ How do you feel now?
- ❖ Breathe out once and open your eyes.
- ❖ Write down your experience.

Lighting your Organs Exercise

- ❖ Move to the Heart.
- ❖ Breathe out once (breathe out a long, slow exhalation through your mouth. Do this once).
- ❖ See, sense and feel that the Sun is becoming smaller and smaller and that it is coming right in front of you at the level of your chest; the Sun is like a small sphere with a diameter of 20 cm.
- ❖ See, sense and feel that your heart is traveling outside of your body right near the small Sun that is in front of you; now your heart is moving inside the small sun and it is filling up with light (wait 30 seconds). Now your heart, that is full of light, is moving back into your body, back to her location; the light is shining from your heart throughout your whole chest area (wait 30 seconds).

- ❖ Breathe out once.
- ❖ See, sense and feel that your liver is traveling outside of your body, right near the small Sun that is in front of you; now your liver is moving inside of the small sun and it is filling up with light (wait 30 seconds). Now your liver is full of light and it is moving back into your body, back to his location; the light is shining from your liver throughout the stomach-liver area (wait 30 seconds).
- ❖ Breathe out once.
- ❖ See, sense and feel that your kidneys are traveling outside of your body right near the small Sun that is in front of you; now your kidneys are moving inside of the small sun and they are filling up with light (wait 30 seconds). Now your kidneys are full of light and they are moving back into your body back to their location; the light is shining from your kidneys throughout the lower back abdominal area (wait 30 seconds).
- ❖ Breathe out once.
- ❖ See, sense and feel that your lungs are traveling outside of your body right near the small Sun that is in front of you; now your lungs are moving inside the small sun and they are filling up with light (wait 30 seconds). Now your lungs are full of light and they are moving back into your body back to their location; the light is shining from your lungs throughout the upper chest area (wait 30 seconds).
- ❖ Breathe out once.
- ❖ See, sense and feel that your brain is traveling outside of your body right near the small Sun that is in front of you; now your brain is moving inside the small sun and it is filling up with light (wait 30 seconds). Now your brain is full of light and it is moving back into your body back to his location; the light is shining from your brain throughout your head area (wait 30 seconds).
- ❖ Now see yourself with your heart, liver, kidneys, lungs and brain shining inside you. How do you feel?

❖ Breathe out once and open your eyes.
❖ Write down your experience.

Lotus Flower Exercise

❖ Move to the Heart.
❖ Breathe out once (breathe out a long, slow exhalation through your mouth. Do this once).
❖ See, sense and feel a Lotus flower right ahead of you, towards the middle of your forehead, at the level of your third eye. Now the Lotus flower is getting bigger and bigger until you sit on it.
❖ See, sense and feel that the Lotus flower is beginning to move upwards, while you are sitting on it; look down and see the buildings, the trees, all the area around; go higher and higher until you are between white clouds that are floating near you. Now move back to the room.
❖ Breathe out once.
❖ See, sense and feel that the Lotus flower is getting smaller and smaller and it is moving down to your first chakra at your perineum level; your first chakra is shining and it is emanating a pleasant fragrance.
❖ See, sense and feel that the Lotus flower is moving up towards your navel chakra right there in the middle of your body, behind the belly button. Your navel chakra is shining and it is emanating a pleasant fragrance.
❖ See, sense and feel that the Lotus flower is moving up towards your upper heart chakra right there in the middle of the chest; your heart chakra is shining and it is emanating a pleasant fragrance.
❖ See, sense and feel that the Lotus flower is moving up towards your third eye chakra; your third eye chakra is shining and it is emanating a pleasant fragrance.
❖ See, sense and feel that the Lotus flower is moving up towards your crown chakra; your crown chakra is shining and it is emanating a pleasant fragrance.

❖ Now see, sense and feel that the Lotus flower is getting bigger and bigger and again and you are sitting on it; how do you feel now?

❖ Breathe out once and open your eyes.

❖ Write down your experience.

Emotional Body Exercise

❖ Move to the Heart.

❖ Breathe out once (breathe out a long, slow exhalation through your mouth. Do this once).

❖ See, sense and feel that your spirit is moving outside and up above your body up and over your own Leonardo sphere.

❖ Look down and see your emotional body as if it is cloud around you and it is spinning clockwise; your emotional body is inside your Leonardo sphere.

❖ With your intention, send light down to your emotional body from up where your spirit is looking down; see, sense and feel how your emotional body, like a vortex, is receiving light inside from up there, and it is cleaning all the energies that do not correspond with your emotional body's energy.

❖ Breathe out once.

❖ See, sense and feel that your emotional body is becoming a white shining cloud around your physical body; feel calm and clean; your emotional traumas are cleaned.

❖ Move your spirit back.

❖ Breathe out once and open your eyes.

❖ Write down your experience.

Waterfall of Light Exercise

❖ Move to the Heart.

❖ Breathe out once (breathe out a long, slow exhalation through your mouth. Do this once).

❖ See that you are sitting in front of two beautiful and serene mountains; in the middle of these two mountains is a waterfall of light.

❖ See that you are getting closer and closer to the waterfall, until you arrive in front of it.

❖ Now step right under the waterfall of light and see, sense, feel and know that the light is cleaning your mental and emotional bodies that are around your physical body.

❖ When the light begins to clean your mental and emotional bodies, feel that your brain is getting cleaner and that you are receiving clarity and peace; know that your mental body is linked with the left brain and your emotional body is linked with the right brain.

❖ Stay there for a minute and feel the light cleaning your bodies and filling your brain with clarity.

❖ Breathe out once and open your eyes.

❖ Write down your experience.

The Seven Components of Healing Exercise

❖ Move to the Heart.

❖ Breathe out once (breathe out a long, slow exhalation through your mouth. Do this once).

❖ See, sense and feel that, here on Earth, we have seven magical components that we may use to heal: energy, movement, water, light, sound, Mother Earth and flowing time.

❖ Know that energy is everything and everything is energy. You are, therefore, you are able to heal yourself with energy.

❖ Know that energy always moves and that life is movement; we are not static; we move and, when we move, the energy moves and heals us.

❖ Know that we are primarily made of water, so if we clean out the water from inside us, by bringing in clean water, we are able to heal ourselves.

❖ Know that light or fire guided by our will and our intention cleans our chakras and heals us.

❖ Know that sound heals; right now, listen to your "inner sound" and let it expand throughout your being; feel how the vibration of the sound heals you.

- ❖ Know that connection with Mother Earth heals; see, sense and feel the healing energy coming from Mother Earth in all your cells; feel that you have to honor who you are as part of Mother Earth; as part of Nature.
- ❖ Know that eternal time is liquid, it flows; see, sense and feel that without time you are eternal; healing happens instantly when you realize that you are eternal.
- ❖ Breathe out once and open your eyes.
- ❖ Write down your experience.

Message from your Ancestors Exercise

- ❖ Move to the Heart.
- ❖ Breathe out once (breathe out a long, slow exhalation through your mouth. Do this once).
- ❖ See, sense and feel that you are walking on a serene mountain trail. You remember this trail, as if you have been there before. Listen to the song of the birds around you. Spring water is flowing down near the trail. Kneel and drink the pure and refreshing water. Wash your eyes with this water.
- ❖ There is a cave right there in front of you; enter the cave and remember when you used to meditate here in your past lives. Feel the connection with this holy place and start meditating there, sitting on a solid rock covered with an old rug.
- ❖ See, sense and feel the bond with the mountain and the Mother Earth.
- ❖ See, sense and feel the relationship with the sky and the Father Universe.
- ❖ See, sense and feel the link with the other workers of light from all over the world and from all over the Universe.
- ❖ Now ask your ancestors to come. Hear what they have to tell you. They give you a message that has to do with your mental body, emotional body and physical body. They tell you how to heal yourself. Hear this message.

❖ One by one, your ancestors leave and you remain there meditating on their message.

❖ See, sense and feel that it is time to let go of any places you have been in, in this existence and that you live only in the now. Feel that the past is over and you have a new energy. You are reborn again; ready to enjoy other beautiful experiences.

❖ Breathe out once and open your eyes.

❖ Write down your experience.

Traveling the Universe Exercise

❖ Move to the Heart

❖ Breathe out once (breathe out a long, slow exhalation through your mouth. Do this once).

❖ Start moving inside the Heart towards the opposite direction facing the door of the Heart.

❖ Shortly, you will arrive to the other side of your Heart, where you will see another door; open that door and step outside.

❖ See, sense and feel that you are in the Universe and that there is a road leading from your heart up to the Sun of our Solar System; take this road and move up towards the Sun; arrive at the Sun and move to the center of It.

❖ See, sense and feel that there is a road leading from the center the Sun to the Galactic Sun - the centre of our Galaxy; take this road and move towards the Galactic Sun; when you have reached the Galactic Sun see, sense and feel thousands of constellations on the left and right side of the road.

❖ See, sense and feel the Galactic Sun; an Archangel of Light is guiding you within this area towards the centre of the Galactic Sun, where the Council of our Galaxy is coordinating all the worlds and Suns; you have now arrived and the Council has a message for you. Hear their message.

❖ They also have a gift for you; take the gift with both hands and thank them for it. The Archangel is now taking you back to our Solar System Sun. From there, return to the door on your own and open the door. Go back into your Heart.

❖ See, sense and feel the importance of the message and the gift that you have received; put the gift down, sit down and begin to meditate.

❖ Breathe out once and open your eyes.

❖ Write down your experience.

The Room Exercise

❖ Move to the Heart.

❖ Breathe out once (breathe out a long, slow exhalation through your mouth. Do this once).

❖ See that you are in a nice place, sitting in a lotus posture.

❖ Look around you, what do you see?

❖ Now see yourself sitting in a small dark room.

❖ Look around at the walls of that room. They are tough, dark, and impenetrable.

❖ How do you feel?

❖ Now see that the walls have been replaced by windows: big, huge, bright windows.

❖ There is no darkness any more. You can see the sky through these windows.

❖ See that the roof of the room has also become a window through which you can see white clouds in the sky.

❖ Now look downwards, where you are sitting. There is no floor any more, it has also been replaced by a window, from which you can see the blue sky.

❖ Feel the light that is shining in towards you.

❖ Feel the light that you are shining outwards.

❖ Breathe out once and open your eyes.

❖ Write down your experience.

The Astral Spine Exercise

❖ Move to the Heart.

❖ Breathe out once (breathe out a long, slow exhalation through your mouth. Do this once).

❖ See that you are in a nice place, sitting in a lotus posture.

❖ See, sense and feel that your spine is transparent, like a tube of light.

❖ Now mentally place the word "OM" down at the base of the spine.

❖ Now move up with your attention and mentally put the word "OM" in the lumbar region, on the same level as the navel.

❖ Now move up with your attention and mentally put the word "OM" in the dorsal area, between the shoulder blades.

❖ Now move up with your attention and mentally put the word "OM" in the middle of the brain.

❖ Finally put the word "OM" up on top of your head.

❖ Feel two invisible strings of light moving up from the base of the spine to the middle of the brain: this is *Pingala* or the solar nerve on the right side of the spine and *Ida* or the lunar nerve on the left side of the spine.

❖ See, sense and feel how the solar nerve brings the esoteric fire up to your brain and how and the lunar nerve brings the esoteric silvery cold energy up, that is located at the base of the spine.

❖ Feel the blissful light in your brain.

❖ Breathe out once and open your eyes.

❖ Write down your experience.

* * *

Practical exercises that can be used in our daily activities with or without meditation

Tibetan Chakra Cleaning Exercise

❖ Move into the Heart.

❖ See yourself, your body there in front of you like a holographic image; see a ray of light extending from your palm chakra (it does not matter which hand) to the first chakra (base chakra) of your holographic image. Clean it with the light that is coming from your palm until you see, sense and feel a beautiful red color and a fragrance of roses coming from there.

❖ Move your palm upwards and clean the second chakra; it is located between the base chakra and the navel. Clean it until you see, sense and feel a beautiful orange color; feel the creation energy being cleaned and released. Feel the fragrance of the orange tree flowers.

❖ Move your palm upwards and clean the third chakra of your holographic image; it is located on the level of the solar plexus, of the stomach. Clean it until you see or feel a beautiful yellow color shining right there, like a small Sun inside your solar plexus. Feel the fragrance of the yellow lemon tree flowers.

❖ Now move your palm upwards and clean the fourth chakra; it is located in the middle of chest area between lungs. Clean the upper heart chakra until you see or feel a beautiful nourishing green color shining right there. Feel the fragrance of the mint green leaves.

❖ Now move your palm upwards and clean the fifth chakra; it is located in the lower throat. Clean it until you see or feel a beautiful blue color, like a summer sky. Feel the fragrance of the linden tree flowers.

❖ Now move your palm upwards and clean the sixth chakra - the third eye; it is located in the middle of the forehead. Clean it until you see or feel a beautiful indigo. Feel the fragrance of the Lila flowers.

❖ Finally move your palm upwards and clean the seventh chakra - the crown chakra. Clean it until you see or feel a beautiful white color. Feel the fragrance of the jasmine flowers.

❖ See, sense and feel that all your chakras from both - your holographic image and your physical body - are cleaned and they are emanating a pleasant fragrance, like a garden of flowers.

❖ Now allow your hologram to merge with your physical body.

Practical Exercise to Let go of Anxiety and Fears and Connect with your Inner Essence

❖ Move into the Heart.

❖ Remember a situation when you were anxious, upset or afraid.

❖ Now observe the rhythm of your breath: the inflow and outflow of your breath; observe how you inhale and exhale without trying to change anything during this process.

❖ You may find that your breathing spontaneously becomes faster or slower deeper or shallow and may even stop from time to time; allow all these changes to happen without resistance or anticipation.

❖ Whenever your attention moves back to the anxiety or the fear from that situation or a sensation in your body (for example whenever your heart beat increases, (gently return your awareness at your breathing).

❖ In a minute or so you will calm down and pass the anxiety and the fear.

The Spiral (Fibonacci) Interior Smile

❖ Move into the Heart.

❖ Realize that inside your Heart is the centre of the Universe and it forms a spiral of light that goes through your main organs in the following order: Heart, Left Lung, Brain, Right Lung, Liver, Right Kidney, Genitals, Left Kidney and Spleen.

It then moves outwards continuing the spiral movement towards the infinite.

❖ Move your attention to your Heart and smile at your heart: practice the Interior Smile with your Heart while you say three times to your Heart: "I love you"; after a few seconds you will feel your Heart vibrating and smiling back at you.

❖ Now move your attention to your Left Lung and smile at your Left Lung: practice the Interior Smile with your Left Lung, while you tell your Left Lung three times "I love you"; after a few seconds you will feel how your Left Lung vibrates and smiles back to you.

❖ Now practice the Interior Smile with your Brain, Right Lung, Liver, Right Kidney, Genitals, Left Kidney and Spleen.

❖ See, sense and feel now that your nine organs are filled with love and light and that they are smiling back at you.

❖ Realize again that the centre of the Universe is inside your Heart and it forms a spiral of light that goes through your main organs in the following order: Heart, Left Lung, Brain, Right Lung, Liver, Right Kidney, Genitals, Left Kidney and Spleen. It moves outwards continuing the spiral movement to the infinite. See and feel this spiral of light moving continuously from your Heart through your organs and proceeding outwards towards the infinite.

Practice this exercise once a day or when you feel disconnected from your Higher Self and from the Universe; when you feel sad and alone.

The Tibetan Hands

❖ Close your eyes and move into the heart.

❖ Rub your hands for a minute relaxing your wrists without opening your eyes.

❖ Sense the parts of your body that are weaker, congested, depleted. Look for the painful areas or for the hot, cold, irregular tingling from electrical charges.

❖ Allow your hands to gently massage the areas of tension, making full contact. Be totally aware of the area of your body where your hands feel areas of tension.

❖ See, sense, feel and know that the white light travels from your hands to the area of pain or tension. See how the area of pain or tension has gradually turned into an area filled with white shining light.

Cleaning With Prana

❖ Move to the Heart.

❖ See, sense and feel how each cell of your body becomes an infinite small window opened to the Universe.

❖ Now inhale and feel how prana is coming inside your body, in all your cells through the opened windows.

❖ See, sense and feel how your entire body has filled with prana.

❖ See, sense and feel that your body is filled with prana now and prana moves from your body to your Leonardo sphere; your Leonardo sphere is now a sphere of prana all around you.

CHAPTER 16

Union with God

Remember that if you want to practice these exercises, you need somebody else to read them to you; reading them or learning them off by heart will cause your mind to take over and you will lose all the positive effects of this exercise.

The Primary Source Exercise

- ❖ Move to the Heart.
- ❖ Breathe out once (breathe out a long, slow exhalation through your mouth. Do this once).
- ❖ See, sense and feel that you are travelling in space from here, from this location directly to the Primary Source.
- ❖ Know that the Primary Source is the source of all that is.
- ❖ How do you see the Primary Source? How does It appear in front of you?
- ❖ Try to see it, feel it and know it.
- ❖ See, sense and feel that Pure Knowledge is in front of you, but that what you see is given by your perception; realize that perception belongs to the world of duality, like our world. Pure Knowledge belongs to Primary Source.
- ❖ See, sense and feel that your perception has no function in the Primary Source, in God. However, the perception is very useful to you; it must become the means for the reinstatement of your awareness and holiness.
- ❖ Breathe out once.
- ❖ See, sense and feel that you are moving inside the Primary Source; how do you feel now?

❖ See, sense and feel that you cannot see anything other than the Primary Source, because you cannot be apart from the Primary Source, from God.

❖ Sense now how enriched you are and feel renewed and revitalized.

❖ Breathe out once and open your eyes.

❖ Write down your experience.

The Healing Prayer Exercise

❖ Move to the Heart.

❖ Breathe out once (breathe out a long, slow exhalation through your mouth. Do this once).

❖ See, sense and feel that you are walking into a forest moving towards a distant light.

❖ Find that you are in an open space in the middle of the forest without trees; a light is coming from above and a perfect circle is formed on the ground.

❖ Stop right in the middle of the circle and feel the light coming from above.

❖ Standing in the middle of the circle, say a healing prayer; let your intuition and your Higher Self give you the words; do not think logically about the prayer nor try to remember any prayers that you know from the past. Allow any healing prayer that you may feel like saying now to come naturally to you.

❖ End your prayer with the words: "*So Be It*".

❖ Breathe out once.

❖ See, sense and feel that your prayer has been heard by God.

❖ See, sense and feel that God's hands are coming from above in the circle of light and they are taking you up. Feel that healing is taking place now as you are travelling up in the hands of God (wait for 2 minutes).

❖ Now Feel God's hands are gently bringing you back in the middle of the circle. Feel as if you have a new life, as if you are reborn again.

- ❖ Breathe out once and open your eyes.
- ❖ Write down your experience.

Heart of Father Universe Exercise

- ❖ Move to the Heart.
- ❖ Breathe out once (breathe out a long, slow exhalation through your mouth. Do this once).
- ❖ See, sense and feel that you are now in the middle of the Universe, right in the Heart of the Universe. Feel how the Heart of the Universe is pulsating all around you; a soft and tender heart beat.
- ❖ See, sense and feel a point of light pulsating inside your heart; the point of light is expanding and contracting with strong rhythmic movements. Feel the waves of light generated by the point of light that is pulsating inside your heart; you can hear a rhythmical throbbing sound coming from the point of light that is pulsating inside your heart.
- ❖ Now gently feel how your pulsation and pulsation of the Heart of the Universe have unified and they have become one; feel the unity of the Hearts and feel only one Heart Beat. The point of light from your heart has connected with the Heart of the Universe.
- ❖ Breathe out once.
- ❖ See, sense and feel that you need to reach the level of total unity with every other person around you, in order to hear the Heart of God; try to bring in the Heart of the Universe all the people with whom you had a conflict or a disagreement and feel the difference between their heart beat and the beat of the Heart of the Universe.
- ❖ Help these people rise up to the same level of unity as you are on now and see, sense and feel them merge with the beat of your heart and of the Heart of the Universe.
- ❖ See, sense and feel that now you are all one person with one heart.

❖ Breathe out once and open your eyes.

❖ Write down your experience.

Cleaning with Colors Exercise

❖ Move to the Heart.

❖ Breathe out once (breathe out a long, slow exhalation through your mouth. Do this once).

❖ See, sense and feel your favorite color like a cloud right in front of you. Feel this color coming towards you from the left, like the wind; feel it going through you, cleaning your emotional body. Now feel an opposite color (whatever an opposite color means to you) coming from the right side, cleaning your mental body. Now feel both colors coming from both directions, going through you, cleaning you completely.

❖ See, sense and feel that you can help clean all your friends, all humanity. Send this two-colored wind from left to right across the planet, cleaning all people on its path. Now send it from the right, cleaning all humanity. Now send it from both sides at once.

❖ See, sense and feel that you are in the middle of the universe; there are stars all around you.

❖ See, sense and feel that there is a giant vacuum cleaner on your left hand side that is taking in all your emotions, issues and negative thoughts. They all go to your left in this vacuum cleaner.

❖ Breathe out once and open your eyes.

❖ Write down your experience.

The Color of God Exercise

❖ Move to the Heart.

❖ Breathe out once (breathe out a long, slow exhalation through your mouth. Do this once).

❖ See, sense and feel that you are on the edge of a mountain and feel that it is the *end of time*. How does it feel? What does "end of time" mean to you? End of time could mean an end to something, such as going into a new dimension or entering a new relationship, anything at all.

❖ Breathe out once.

❖ See, sense and feel the Color of God. How does the Color of God appear to you? This color is approaching you like a cloud, it envelopes you and it enters into you. You become this color. Your stomach, liver, eyes, mental and emotional bodies are this color. Your physical body is this color.

❖ See, sense and feel that your physical, emotional body and mental body are the same; they have the same color; the Color of God. They are in harmony.

❖ Breathe out once.

❖ See, sense and feel that you are infinite. Time does not exist. Bring the infinity sign inside you and expand yourself with this sign all over the Universe. Feel that you are the infinite spirit, the Mother. See, sense and feel everything and all in the Universe.

❖ Breathe out once and open your eyes.

❖ Write down your experience.

The Green Field Exercise

❖ Move to the Heart.

❖ Breathe out once (breathe out a long, slow exhalation through your mouth. Do this once).

❖ See, sense and feel the taste of lemon in your mouth. Associate lemon with either your emotional or your mental body. Now feel the taste of honey in your mouth, associate it with the other body. Now mix them together. How do you feel?

❖ Breathe out once.

❖ See, sense and feel that you are walking through a green field together with all of your friends. Try to see, sense and feel the direction you are walking in: north, east, south or west. Where is the sun?

❖ Breathe out once.

❖ See, sense and feel now that the green grass field is inside you. How do you feel? In that same green field, realize that you are alone. How do you feel now? Again feel that the green grass is inside you. If you feel sad and lonely, bring your friends back; otherwise, if you feel detached, continue walking alone.

❖ See, sense and feel that we are all one. Look inside and see the green field and realize that it is empty; you are the green field now.

❖ Breathe out once and open your eyes.

❖ Write down your experience.

The Great Masters Exercise

❖ Move to the Heart.

❖ Breathe out once (breathe out a long, slow exhalation through your mouth. Do this once).

❖ See, sense and feel that you were alive more than 2000 years ago. You are in a crowd watching Jesus speak. You are one of his disciples. He is giving you a lesson about unconditional love and he is behaving towards your neighbor in the same manner you would behave towards yourself. Listen to what Jesus has to say and allow all the feelings that arise in you to settle within you; accept yourself and feel love for yourself.

❖ Breathe out once.

❖ See, sense and feel that you are sitting in a lotus posture in front of Buddha over 2500 years ago. You are one of his disciples. He is giving you a lesson about compassion and understanding people around you. Listen to Buddha and allow all the feelings that arise in you to settle within you.

❖ Breathe out once.

❖ See, sense and feel that you are a Master; there are people around you. You are sending them love and energy and you are teaching them a lesson about innocence. You are telling them that they have no enemy other than themselves and teach them to beware of the temptation to perceive themselves as being unfairly treated. Teach them that innocence cannot be obtained by handing out guilt to someone else.

❖ Breathe out once and open your eyes.
❖ Write down your experience.

The Most Familiar Place Exercise

❖ Move to the Heart.
❖ Breathe out once (breathe out a long, slow exhalation through your mouth. Do this once).
❖ See, sense and feel that you are in the middle of your most familiar and favorite room of your childhood. Start cleaning the room, from right to the left. Take a vacuum cleaner and clean the room, the bed, the floor, the desk. Now push everything, including all the furniture, out of the room to the left.
❖ Breathe out once.
❖ See, sense and feel that you are in the middle of your most familiar and favorite place in nature. Start cleaning the place; the grass or the tree or the lake water or the sky. Push all pollution and radiation to the left until it is all clean.
❖ See, sense and feel that you are in the middle of your most familiar and favorite place in the Universe; it might be a star, a planet, a galaxy. Try to feel the energy there and relax. Just enjoy the place.
❖ Breathe out once and open your eyes.
❖ Write down your experience.

The Ocean Masters Exercise

❖ Move to the Heart.
❖ Breathe out once (breathe out a long, slow exhalation through your mouth. Do this once).
❖ See, sense and feel that you are meditating on a beautiful white sandy beach near the beautiful blue and crystal clear ocean; you can hear the pleasant sound of the waves and a soft breeze is gently touching your face.

❖ Hear the call of the Dolphins and the Whales; this call is vibrating in your heart.

❖ Get up and go into the water. Start swimming into the ocean; the dolphins and whales are coming and taking you to the middle of the ocean. Meditate there with their Master Dolphin and Master Whale who are waiting for you.

❖ The Master Dolphin has a message for you. Hear this message. He has a gift for you too; take the gift.

❖ The Master Whale has a message for you. Hear this message. She has a gift for you too.

❖ Now take the gifts with you and continue swimming back to the shore.

❖ Go back to the white sandy beach and put the gifts down in front of you; the gifts transform in something else; what are they now?

❖ Now, there on the beach, close your eyes and meditate on the message given to you by the Master Dolphin and Master Whale.

❖ Breathe out once and open your eyes.

❖ Write down your experience.

The Healing Exercise

❖ Move to the Heart.

❖ Breathe out once (breathe out a long, slow exhalation through your mouth. Do this once).

❖ See, sense and feel that healing has been accomplished in the moment when you no longer see any value in pain; do that now and clear the idea of pain out of you.

❖ See, sense and feel that any area of pain in your body has healed instantly. See that pain is of no value and suffering is futile; it is useless.

❖ Breathe out once.

❖ See and sense that the whole humanity feels the same way as you do now: the pain and suffering vanish out of each person on this planet.

❖ Breathe out once and open your eyes.

❖ Write down your experience.

The Breathing Exercise

❖ Move to the Heart.

❖ Breathe out once (breathe out a long, slow exhalation through your mouth. Do this once).

❖ See, sense and feel that your body is part of the universe; everything in the body is part of the universe.

❖ See, sense and feel that your breath is a bridge between your body and the universe; one end of this bridge is in your body, while the other is outside in nothingness.

❖ Breathe out once.

❖ See, sense and feel that you know half of bridge that is inside your body, but you do not know the other half of the bridge; where does your breath go?

❖ See, sense and feel that if you were to know the other half of the bridge, you would suddenly know nothingness; you would be transformed and know the other dimension. Try to sense where your breath goes; see the nothingness.

❖ See, sense and feel that if you were to stop your breath, you would stop your mind. Your breath and your mind are inter-related; stop your breath for three seconds and realize that your mind has stopped too.

❖ Breathe out once and open your eyes.

❖ Write down your experience.

The Creation Exercise

❖ Move to the Heart.

❖ Breathe out once (breathe out a long, slow exhalation through your mouth. Do this once).

❖ See, sense and feel that anything you create inside the heart is of much greater value than what you create inside your brain.

❖ See an image now of a creation from your heart: feel the vibration of this creation. See, sense and feel the energy coming from this image; a unity field is surrounding this creation and you feel safe and protected.

❖ Now see an image of a creation from your brain; feel the vibration of this creation.

❖ Breathe out once.

❖ See, sense and feel how the world would be if all humanity created only from the heart.

❖ Breathe out once and open your eyes.

❖ Write down your experience.

The Inner Light Exercise

❖ Move to the Heart.

❖ Breathe out once (breathe out a long, slow exhalation through your mouth. Do this once).

❖ See, sense and feel that there is a light in you that the world cannot recognize; open your eyes within and see this light. Realize that if you use the eyes of the world you will not see the light within; you need to use your inner vision, your inner eyes.

❖ See, sense and feel that this inner light is a reflection of God's love and light.

❖ Breathe out once.

❖ See, sense and feel that your inner light is projecting outside and you can see the world shining in innocence and blessed with divine clarity and love.

❖ See, sense and feel that the inner light is keeping you safe from every form of danger and pain.

❖ Breathe out once.

❖ See, sense and feel how all people see their inner light and that all people's minds have been restored and re-established completely with this love and light.

❖ Breathe out once and open your eyes.

❖ Write down your experience.

The Love of God Exercise

- ❖ Move to the Heart.
- ❖ Breathe out once (breathe out a long, slow exhalation through your mouth. Do this once).
- ❖ See, sense and feel that the love of God is everywhere: you can see it, smell it, touch it and feel it all around you. The love of God is like an ocean and you are living in this ocean.
- ❖ Breathe out once.
- ❖ See, sense and feel that what is not love, is always fear and nothing else.
- ❖ See, sense and feel that confusing sacrificing for love is so deep, that you are unable to perceive love without sacrifice; see that this sacrifice is fear, not love.
- ❖ See, sense and feel that you have the gift of freedom; you do not need to sacrifice anything. See that you are completely free. Feel the Love of God within you and around you.
- ❖ Breathe out once and open your eyes.
- ❖ Write down your experience.

The Teachers of God Exercise

- ❖ Move to the Heart.
- ❖ Breathe out once (breathe out a long, slow exhalation through your mouth. Do this once).
- ❖ See, sense and feel that atonement and reconciliation correct illusions, not truth; truth does not need to be corrected.
- ❖ See, sense and feel that there is a group of teachers that have a special role in the reconciliation plan; the Teachers of God.
- ❖ See, sense and feel the nine characteristics of the advanced Teachers of God: open-mindedness, generosity, patience, tolerance, joy, gentleness, honesty, trust and unconditional love.
- ❖ Breathe out once.
- ❖ See, sense and feel that the main function of the Teachers of God is to bring true learning to the world; their function is

to unlearn what we think is true, what we think is real and to teach true learning.

❖ See, sense and feel that part of their function is to give complete forgiveness to the world; to teach how we have to let go of all things that prevent forgiveness.

❖ Breathe out once.

❖ See, sense and feel that you are one of the Teachers of God; see which of the nine characteristics of the advanced Teachers of God are mirrored in yourself now (open-mindedness, generosity, patience, tolerance, joy, gentleness, honesty, trust and unconditional love).

❖ Breathe out once and open your eyes.

❖ Write down your experience.

The Goal of Truth Exercise

❖ Move to the Heart.

❖ Breathe out once (breathe out a long, slow exhalation through your mouth. Do this once).

❖ See, sense and feel that whenever you are uncertain in your life, you need a clarification of your goal. The heart will give you your goal; see, sense and feel your goal here on this world. Call it the goal of truth (two minutes). When you see, sense and feel your goal of truth you will experience peace; a divine peace.

❖ See, sense and feel that the only characteristics required by the goal of truth are faith and trust.

❖ Breathe out once.

❖ See, sense and feel that what you want to happen simply constitutes a situation as a means to achieve your goal of truth.

❖ See now how many situations in your life were in accordance with your goal of truth; understand that your life is fragmented and it is not in unity, because you do not have a goal of truth.

- ❖ Remember your goal of truth and use it whenever you feel conflict and fragmentation around you.
- ❖ Breathe out once and open your eyes.
- ❖ Write down your experience.

The Master Initiation Exercise

- ❖ Move to the Heart.
- ❖ Breathe out once (breathe out a long, slow exhalation through your mouth. Do this once).
- ❖ See, sense and feel that you are in front of your Master and feel that he is helping you to awaken; stop fighting with yourself and open the door of your heart. Do not close up. Do not be afraid.
- ❖ See, sense and feel that you are vulnerable; the Master can enter you. You are humble, surrendered and open to receive.
- ❖ Breathe out once.
- ❖ See, sense and feel that, in order to be initiated, you must surrender yourself totally and let the energy flow down from the Master to you; this energy flows down from the Master to anyone who is receptive, humble and surrendered.
- ❖ See, sense and feel that you are a valley and the Master is a peak of a mountain; see a deep transfer of energy from the Master to you, just like the water flows from the peak of the mountain down to the beautiful valley. Let the purest energy come to you; you have a receptive attitude, a deep humbleness and you start to receive energy and knowledge from the Master (2 minutes).
- ❖ See, sense and feel that initiation is a transfer of inner energy and if you are open and receptive, the Master can enter your heart and transform you, clean you and clear your mind.
- ❖ Breathe out once.
- ❖ See, sense and feel that the humanity cannot be initiated; it cannot be awakened, because it does not trust and it sets conditions.

❖ See, sense and feel that once humanity opens its heart, the Masters can help it and it can awaken, just as you did.

❖ Breathe out once and open your eyes.

❖ Write down your experience.

The Sounds of God Exercise

❖ Move to the Heart.

❖ Breathe out once (breathe out a long, slow exhalation through your mouth. Do this once).

❖ See, sense and feel that your Master is giving you a sound that resonates with your energy; this sound is a key that unlocks the energy of your heart.

❖ Start chanting this sound inside your heart and see, sense and feel that this entire energy has begun to move around you like a rainbow of colors and sounds (one minute).

❖ Remember that this mantra is your personal sound and it belongs only to you; it cannot be given to anyone else and you promise your Master to keep it just for you.

❖ Breathe out once.

❖ See, sense and feel that life everywhere has a deep, energetic sound inside that unlocks the energy around; any flower, any tree, and animal, any element: water, fire, wind. Listen to these sounds and let them fill your heart.

❖ See, sense and feel the sound of Mother Earth; let it fill your heart too.

❖ See, sense and feel the sound of Father Sun and realize that all around us is a giant symphony of God' sounds.

❖ Breathe out once.

❖ See, sense and feel that the Universe is chanting the sound AUM. Feel each letter sound: first the 'A', then the 'U' and finally the 'M' and let them enter your heart.

❖ Breathe out once and open your eyes.

❖ Write down your experience.

The Universal Unity Exercise

- ❖ Move to the Heart.
- ❖ Breathe out once (breathe out a long, slow exhalation through your mouth. Do this once).
- ❖ See, sense and feel that God is unity; even if you live in a material and physical world. See, sense and feel the unity of the Universe; how do you perceive the unity of the Universe?
- ❖ Next, see, sense and feel that you are part of this unity. How do you feel?
- ❖ Breathe out once.
- ❖ See, sense and feel the Isle of Light in the middle of the Universe where The Unqualified Absolute upholds the physical universe.
- ❖ See, sense and feel that the Isle of Light is the actual source of all material universes: past, present and future.
- ❖ See, sense and feel that every impulse of every electron of your body, thought or spirit is an acting unit in the whole Universe.
- ❖ Breathe out once and open your eyes.
- ❖ Write down your experience.

The Acceptance Exercise

- ❖ Move to the Heart.
- ❖ Breathe out once (breathe out a long, slow exhalation through your mouth. Do this once).
- ❖ See, sense and feel that life is divided into two aspects: one is the seen world and the other is the unseen, the hidden manifestation of the world. Realize that there is no contradiction between those two aspects and they are just two aspects of the same existence.
- ❖ See, sense and feel that, because you cannot see the whole, the world appears to be something which is against divinity and you have to fight the world to reach the divine aspect inside of you.

❖ See, sense and feel that the whole is whole and the part that you see is the world and the part that is hidden is the divine, or God. This part, however, is here and now. You do not need to travel to find it; you only need to open your eyes and see it; you only need to awaken.

❖ See, sense and feel that if you do not accept the world totally, then you are tense and divided, in conflict and fear.

❖ See, sense and feel that you do not need to be in favor of the world or against the world; you only need to accept it as it is. Do that now: accept the world as it is and you will be instantly transformed. You will see, sense and feel the unseen part, the divinity. All your energy will be relieved and not engaged in conflicts anymore.

❖ Accept your fate, whatever it is and let yourself flow like a river and change, just as the water does when it flows down into the ocean.

❖ Breathe out once and open your eyes.

❖ Write down your experience.

The Trinity Exercise

❖ Move to the Heart.

❖ Breathe out once (breathe out a long, slow exhalation through your mouth. Do this once).

❖ See, sense and feel the three personalizations of God: the Universal Father, the Eternal Son and the Infinite Spirit. Realize that on sub-infinite levels there are three Absolutes, but in infinity they appear to be **ONE**.

❖ See, sense and feel the three characteristics of each being of the Universe: truth, beauty and goodness. Then see, sense and feel that these characteristics are bringing you closer to God; they are helping you perceive God in your mind, matter and spirit.

❖ Finally see, sense and feel that, for you, truth, beauty and goodness embrace the full revelation of divinity reality.

❖ Breathe out once.

❖ See, sense and feel what Jesus explained to the twelve Apostles around him when he said: "*He who would be greatest among you, let him become server of all*". Furthermore, see, sense and feel why it is that, when you become the highest level of consciousness and you are like a light, you need to help others who are lost in darkness.

❖ See, sense and feel that love is desire to do good onto others.

❖ See, sense and feel how many times in your life you did good onto others and realized that you created love when you did all these acts.

❖ Breathe out once and open your eyes.

❖ Write down your experience.

* * *

Practical exercises that can be used in our daily activities with or without doing a meditation.

Reviewing your Life's Best Moments Meditation

❖ Use your favorite music meditation for this exercise, a song that keeps you in alpha waves

❖ Move to the Heart.

❖ Breathe out once (breathe out a long, slow exhalation through your mouth. Do this once).

❖ See yourself as you are today, now, in this moment.

❖ Rewind your life from this moment back to the moment when you were born and see, sense and feel your life's best moments.

❖ Try not to be attached to it; just see it again as if you are watching a movie and observe how you were at that moment.

❖ How do you feel now that you have seen your life's best moments?

❖ Practice this exercise once a week to recharge your energy.

God's Unity Consciousness Exercise

* ❖ Practical Exercise to dissolve yourself into God's Unity Consciousness
* ❖ Inhale into the Heart; open the heart and feel the prana coming there **into your physical heart**.
* ❖ This is a very good exercise to connect with your inner essence and feel God inside of you.
* ❖ This is to be practiced whenever you feel like it, but at least 5 minutes before falling asleep. It will help you dream consciously after a few weeks of practicing.

Forgiveness Meditation

Use your favorite music meditation for this exercise, a song that keeps you in alpha waves

* ❖ Move to the Heart.
* ❖ Breathe out once (breathe out a long, slow exhalation through your mouth. Do this once).
* ❖ Now, in your heart, bring the image and energy of those with whom you had an issue or a conflict and remember that we are all the same. If the Creator made you, then the Creator has also certainly made the people with whom you were in conflict.
* ❖ Practice forgiveness and understanding; whenever you bring a person into your heart, look into the eyes of that person and say to him or her: "*I forgive you* [the name of person]; after this step, see that you are in your heart and say to yourself: "*I forgive myself*".
* ❖ Remember that a conflict is always duality and as much as we want to believe that fault lies with others, there are karmic links from this life or past lives that connect us deeply with these persons. Therefore, you need to forgive yourself too.

Union with God through Prayer (Divine Prayer)
- ❖ Move into the Heart.
- ❖ Allow any prayer that comes to you in a natural way to manifest in your heart and say that prayer there in your Heart.
- ❖ See, sense, feel and know that the Prayer is heard by God.

The Three Centers Cleaning Meditation
- ❖ Move into the Heart.
- ❖ Move your attention behind your navel where the centre of the first sphere of our body is: the centre of being.
- ❖ Breathe-in there as if you are filling a bottle with water.
- ❖ In a consciousness way, bring prana there and see the sphere filled with prana.
- ❖ There are ten rays of light going from the centre of the first sphere outside, touching the circumference of the sphere, the sphere's margin.
- ❖ Turn your attention to the sphere of the heart: the second sphere of your body where you have your feeling centre.
- ❖ Breathe-in there as if you are filling a bottle with water.
- ❖ In a consciousness way, bring prana there and see the sphere filled with prana.
- ❖ There are ten rays of light going outwards from the centre of the sphere of the heart, touching the circumference of the sphere, the sphere's margin.
- ❖ Turn your attention now to the third sphere; the knowledge sphere: the sphere of the third eye that is up in the middle of your brain on a straight line from your forehead.
- ❖ See, sense and feel your third eye right in the middle of the forehead and focus on it.
- ❖ Now turn your breath flow from your heart centre to the middle of your brain and feel that your head is filled with prana, with light.

❖ There are eight rays of light going outwards from the centre of the sphere of the head, touching the circumference of the sphere, the sphere's margin.

❖ See, sense and feel that all your three spheres are filled with light and prana.

❖ Practice this meditation once a week or as many times as possible: it helps to centre yourself.

The Gratitude Exercise

❖ Move into the Heart.

❖ See, sense and feel the word *"Gratitude"* in front of you written in words made of pure golden light; what do you experience when you see these words in front of you?

❖ Once a month and for three days, see the word "Gratitude" in front of you before doing an activity; any activity, even walking or eating.

❖ See, sense and feel gratitude for each step you take, each piece of bread or slice of apple you eat, each word you say and hear.

❖ Feel the unconditional love behind each activity, fill your heart and soul with it and let it stay there.

❖ Before falling asleep, feel gratitude for the day that has passed and, in the morning, feel gratitude that you are starting a new day.

Empty your Mind Exercise

❖ Move into the Heart.

❖ See, sense and feel that your mind is a blue sky and your thoughts are white clouds gently moving in it.

❖ With your intention, move the thoughts with a soft wind; the wind is gently blowing from left to right.

Another Way of Looking at the World Exercise

To be practiced for two days in row.

First Day (three sessions of 30 minutes)

This exercise explains why you can see all purpose in everything.

Move into the Heart every morning before you start your day.

This exercise is telling us that God is in everything we see and feel.

So, for 30 minutes, three times a day, begin by repeating the idea and applying it on randomly chosen subjects, naming each one specifically and clearly. You can begin with what you see around you:

God is in this tree.

God is in this computer.

God is in this door.

God is in this apple.

God is in this person (say the name of the person).

If you focus and do this without thinking of something else, you should feel peace and very calm and have the sense that we are all one.

Second Day (three sessions of 30 minutes)

This exercise continues the idea from the previous exercise and adds another dimension to it.

Move into the Heart every morning before you start your day.

This exercise is telling us that God is the light in which we see and feel everything.

So, again for 30 minutes, three times a day, begin by repeating the idea and applying it on randomly chosen subjects:

God is the light in which I see this tree.

God is the light in which I see this computer.

God is the light in which I see this apple.

God is the light in which I see this person.

Whenever you have a chance during the day, close your eyes a couple of times and repeat to yourself: *"God is the light in which I see and feel everything"*.

If you focus and do this without thinking of something else, you should feel peace and very calm and have the sense that we are all made of **LIGHT**.

PART FIVE

This Now is Eternity

THIS NOW IS ETERNITY

Time became fluid. There was no past, present or future. There was just an eternal now.

Days and months passed by, but I intuitively knew that the day would come when the Masters would ask me to return back to the world.

It was a beautiful summer day and the sun was gently touching our faces.

"It is time now, dear Tenzin," Karma Dorje told me as he looked into my eyes.

I did not ask questions. I knew what he was referring to.

Tenzin Dhargey completed the thought of the other Master and said "You are ready."

I could also feel the presence of *Dharmapala* -The Protector- of the monastery.

"Our Lama Master, Tenzin Tashi, sends you love and blessings. He says that you have remembered who you really are," Karma Dorje said.

I was quiet. I knew they were right.

"Remember, dear Tenzin, that there is no past or future. There is just now, here. Wherever you are, when you realize the power of now, you are with us. All we have is an everlasting now. This now is eternity."

I looked into their eyes and saw that they were eternity. They were pure and empty of past burdens and future thoughts.

I smiled and they smiled back.

Indeed, this *now* is all we have.

This now is eternity.

PART SIX

List of Meditations

LIST OF MEDITATIONS

Jungney -the Origin- Breathing Meditation .... Chapter 2

The **first step** is to keep a good meditation posture with a straight back and relaxed shoulders. In that position, your chin usually moves slightly, just a little bit, towards your neck; to a small degree. Part of the first step is to keep your tongue up and touching the roof of your mouth.

The **second step** is to close your eyes and slightly cross them looking up towards the middle of your forehead, at the opening of your third eye.

And the **third, and last step**, is to start breathing all the way down to your navel area.

Tinley -*the Enlightened*- Meditation .... Chapter 2

The **first step** is to focus on the third eye, looking up with eyes slightly crossed, while your tongue touches the roof of the mouth - at any point of the roof.

The **second step** is to see yourself as an empty vessel and breathe prana down, seeing how you, the empty vessel, are filling up from the bottom upwards, just as if you are filling up a glass of water.

The **last step** is to imagine that the essence of prana is showering from the top of your head: a shower of light falling down from the top of your head over your face, your back, your hands, all over.

Thokmay -*the Unobstructed*- Meditation .... Chapter 3

So the **first step** is to cover your eyes or stay in a perfectly dark room with your eyes and mouth closed and your ears closed with some ear plugs.

Again remember to keep your tongue connected with the roof of your mouth and slightly cross your eyes looking up towards the middle of your forehead.

The **second step** is to be aware, at that time of breathing when you are in between the exhalation and the inhalation. Breathe in gently and deeply at your navel center and breathe out slowly, slowly, until your body and your lungs are empty. Then stay like that for a few seconds and be aware of that time when you are in between your exhalation and the next inhalation, when your breathing stops and your nostrils stop working; when they are not bringing anything inside.

Ngodup -*the Attainment*- **Meditation** .... Chapter 3

Remember to keep the tongue gently touching the roof of the mouth and slightly cross your eyes looking up towards the middle of your forehead.

The **first step** is to be aware of your five main centers (chakras): perineum, navel, heart, third eye and top of the head (crown chakra).

The **second step** is to breathe in through your nostrils down to your perineum and, as you breathe-in, go up from the perineum to the top of the head, passing through all 5 centers. As you breathe-in, count each center you are passing through: when you are in the perineum chakra, say 'one', when you are in navel chakra say 'two', all the way up until you arrive to the top of the head, where you say 'five'.

You can use also colors: when you are in the perineum chakra say 'red'. When you are in the navel chakra say 'orange', for the heart chakra 'green', for third eye 'indigo' and for crown chakra 'white'.

The **next step** is to exhale from the top of the head down to perineum using the same route. Again when you go down and pass through each chakra count 'five-four-three-two-one' or say 'white-indigo-green-orange-red'.

Then stay for a few seconds in the perineum between your exhalation and the next inhalation, when your breathing stops and your nostrils stop working.

Do this five times. Repeat it as many times as you wish, but always in sets of five.

Your consciousness is usually situated in the head center and from there you can look down inside your body, as if you are on top of our monastery, which is on top of the mountain. From up there, in that small room that is right on top of the monastery, start moving down the spiral stairs. So up there in the room is your head and you -your consciousness- moves down using the spiral stairs and stops right in front of the heart. I mean your physical heart.

There you can see a door. Open that door and enter your heart where you will see a real universe. The Heart Universe! The Heart World! You might see stars, or pyramids, or rooms, or forests and waterfalls, anything.

Keep the tip of your tongue on the roof of the mouth and slightly cross your eyes looking up towards the middle of your forehead.

The first step is to understand that your consciousness is usually situated in the head center and from there you can look down inside your body, as if you are on top of our monastery, which is on top of the mountain. From up there, in that small room that is right on top of the monastery, start moving down the spiral stairs. So up there in the room is your head and you -your consciousness- moves down using the spiral stairs and stops right in front of the heart. I mean your physical heart.

There you can see a door. Open that door and enter your heart where you will see a real universe. The Heart Universe! The Heart World! You might see stars, or pyramids, or rooms, or forests and waterfalls, anything.

The second step is to start breathing down to your navel center and bring prana there. Do it for a couple of minutes. Remember to keep the tongue gently touching the roof of the mouth throughout the meditation and to slightly cross your eyes looking up towards the middle of your forehead.

The third, and the last step, is to move your prana by breathing from your navel center to your third eye center; to your middle forehead area, towards where you are looking. This step can take more minutes; sometimes even an hour. During this last step, you will feel that, as you breathe, that prana opens a tunnel and a vibration begins to pulsate there.

Love Meditation ....Chapter 4

This meditation must be practiced by both lovers for five minutes, five hours, five days, five weeks or five months. Start first with five minutes and do it for one week.

First step: feel reverence in the presence of your lover. See the divine in him or in her. Feel God in him or her. Make your relationship a sacred state.

Second step: suddenly will feel that you are one and deep down a wall has broken. Your bodies cannot separate you; you become one in harmony and you completely forget that you are there.

Mother Earth Meditation......................................Chapter 5

The first step is to keep a good meditation posture with a straight back and relaxed shoulders. Keep the tip of your tongue on the roof of the mouth, close your eyes and slightly cross them looking up towards the opening of your third eye. Start breathing all the way down to your navel area. Remember to move into the heart (the first step from Third Eye Meditation).

The second step is to see yourself in the middle of nature and that you are becoming part of Mother Earth: you can feel, for example, that you become a flower or a tree: feel yourself grounded in the earth with strong and powerful roots that go deep down inside Mother Earth. Feel yourself actually becoming Earth herself.

Inhale and feel that your body is part of the Divine Mother Earth. Feel that your breath is the same as Mother Earth's breath, your pulse is the same as Mother Earth's pulse; your heart is the same as Mother Earth's heart.

Feel that you are earth. Feel that you are water. Feel that you are wood.

Feel that you are fire. Feel that you are metal. Feel that you are earth, water, wood, fire and metal: the five elements of the Universe.

The third step is to feel that you are really big, as Mother Earth, and that you are orbiting around the Sun. You can feel Venus behind you and Mars in front of you. You can feel the whole Universe around you.

The Inner Self Meditation .... Chapter 6

The first step is to keep a good meditation posture with a straight back and relaxed shoulders. Keep the tip of your tongue on the roof of the mouth, close your eyes and slightly cross them looking up towards the opening of your third eye. Start breathing all the way down to your navel area. Remember to move into the heart (the first step from the Third Eye meditation). Again, feel the vibration of the Divine Mother Earth. With your intention move your Spirit inside your heart and, with your inner vision, see two sacred, tranquil and serene mountains in front of you. Between the mountains there is a beautiful waterfall. At the bottom of the mountains is a meadow with flowers and birds; it is like paradise.

Sit there with your legs crossed in a perfect lotus posture and relax your mind and body. When you feel ready to call you Inner Self, do it gently and use all your intention. Your Inner Self will come to you in any form possible: it may be a human being, an angel, a thought, a ray of light, a celestial being, a geometrical form like a pyramid, a crystal; anything.

STOP Method .... Chapter 6

If you can stop yourself when your mind is in the middle of the process, then you are out of the box. It is easy when you do it without any premeditation. Do not program yourself to stop in the middle of thinking. Of course, it would be better if you had a friend say 'STOP' without warning and so you would have to stop immediately from whatever it is that you are doing.

You need to stop thinking, to stop working. You even need to stop breathing.

But remember that it needs to be authentic: if it is not authentic it will not work. And the simple way is to start reducing your repetitive habits. If you habitually tend to use a word, a gesture or a particular phrase, you need to drop it. Any habit that is stopped suddenly brings inner silence and it quietens your mind.

For example, if you tend to nod your head when you say a sentence, and you do it in order to emphasize your words, then try to say the words without nodding your head. If you can do that, then suddenly you will feel a certain freedom, a certain veil lifting from your eyes.

Any mechanical response should be stopped; a mechanical response, a habit, is a trick of the mind. If you can break down these habits, then the mind disappears for a moment and you will be able to see. It is easy, but you need to persevere; you need to repeat this method as many times as possible.

Statue Meditation' .... Chapter 6

The **first step** is to close your eyes and relax your entire body. You can do this by sitting in a chair or lying down.

The **second step** is to feel that you are just a stone; you cannot move at all. You are like a statue. You cannot move your hands; you cannot open your eyes. Any pain you have in your body disappears. You are like dead. Suddenly everything around you will disappear: the chair or the bed, the room, the whole world will vanish. You will become centered in yourself and your mind will have stopped.

The Food Combination Rules .... Chapter 7

Eggs should never be combined with fish or meat.

There is a risk if combined with cheese, wheat starch products (bread, pasta, potatoes, rice, corn) and nuts or seeds.

Eggs go very well with fresh vegetables.

Meat should never be combined with fish, eggs, cheese or wheat starch products.

There is a risk if combined with nuts and seeds.

Meat goes very well just with fresh vegetables.

Fish should never be combined with eggs, meat and cheese.

There is a risk if combined with nuts and seeds.

Fish goes very well with fresh vegetables and wheat starch products.

Cheese should never be combined with fish and meat.

There is a risk if combined with eggs.

Cheese goes very well with fresh vegetables, wheat starch products, nuts and seeds.

Wheat starch products should never be combined with meat.

There is a risk if combined with eggs.

Wheat starch products go very well with fresh vegetables, cheese, fish, nuts and seeds.

Fresh vegetables go well with any product.

Fruit goes alone; it is not combined with anything.

Fruit alone constitutes a meal!

Inner Light Meditation .... Chapter 8

The first step is to either go into a dark room and close your eyes or simply cover your eyes with a sleeping mask. Be sure there is no light coming in.

When your face has completely relaxed, "look" around and within, keeping your eyes closed, and without moving either head or eyes. Imagine yourself in the middle of darkness. See, sense and feel the darkness; feel it inside of you. Darkness will deeply relax you. Darkness will be outside and inside of you. Feel and love the darkness, as you do this exercise.

Suddenly, in the middle of this darkness, a light will appear.

Inner Vibration Meditation ....Chapter 8

❖ Move into the Heart and keep the tongue touching the roof of the mouth

❖ Send your love to Mother Earth.

❖ Visualize the five main chakras: the perineum chakra, the navel chakra, the heart chakra, the third eye chakra, the crown chakra; Go to each of them and feel them; each chakra has a feeling, a sensation; it provides a specific perception. When you do this exercise, visualize at each chakra the image and the energy of a Master whom you know and love. Stay at each chakra for just 2-3 seconds. Feel it and see the image of the Master. After you arrive at the crown chakra, go back to the first chakra using the backward route: fifth chakra, fourth, third, second and first. When you do the backward route, see, sense and feel the Masters again in each chakra.

❖ Start breathing down to the first chakra; the perineum chakra. Inhale normally, but give out a long and slow exhalation. After that, stay for 3-4 seconds in that time when you are in between the exhalation and the next inhalation. Do this exercise three times. There is a specific way to inhale for the first chakra. It is as if you are filling a bottle with water. Try to visualize that the flow of air, which is brought through your nostrils, is going down to the first chakra. Do this three times.

❖ Move your attention to the second chakra; the navel chakra. Follow the same procedure as with the first chakra: inhale normally, but give out a long and slow exhalation. After that, stay for 3-4 seconds in that time when you are in between the exhalation and the next inhalation. Do this three times. There is a specific way to inhale for the second chakra. It is the same as with the first chakra: as if you are pouring water into a bottle. Try to visualize that the flow of air, which is brought through your nostrils, is going down to the navel chakra. Do this three times.

❖ Move your attention to the third chakra: the heart chakra, in the middle of your chest area. Follow the same procedure as with the first two chakras. Do this three times.

❖ Move your attention to the fourth chakra: the third eye chakra in the middle of your forehead. Follow the same procedure as with the first three chakras, but now, breathe in to the third eye: see, sense and feel that the flow of prana is going from the nostrils directly to the third eye. Do this three times.

❖ Move your attention to the fifth chakra: the crown chakra, right on top of your head, where the fontanel is. Follow the same procedure as with the other four chakras.

❖ See, sense and feel that the flow of prana is going from the nostrils directly to the third eye. Do this three times.

❖ Go back now from the fifth chakra down to the first chakra, following the same breathing technique.

❖ Place one palm over the other (males place their right palm over the left and females place their left palm over the right) and place them on the navel. Start doing gently anti-clockwise circles over it. Do this 27 times.

❖ Now put your palms over your chest and do the same exercise for the heart center.

❖ Then, place your palms over the middle of your forehead and do the same exercise for the third eye center.

❖ Stay there for a few minutes and feel the three centers vibrate (navel, heart and third eye).

This is Just a Dream Exercise .... Chapter 9

Whatever you do, remember this is just a dream. While you eat, walk, read or watch something, say to yourself: *'this is a dream'*. While you are awake, allow your mind to remember, without interruption, that everything, all that exists around you, is a dream.

You only need to constantly and continuously remember, for a period of three months, that whatever you do, it is just a dream. If you can do this for three months straight, then the old pattern of the mind will begin to dissolve.

If you can constantly awaken yourself and remind yourself continuously that *'this is a dream'* for three consecutive months, then one night during the fourth month, while you are dreaming, you will suddenly remember that 'this is a dream'.

This is a very powerful tool to destroy the dreaming process; to remain aware, vigilant and conscious all the time.

When you see a car, say: *'this is a dream'*. While slicing bread in the morning, say: *'this is a dream'*. While cleaning your house say: *'this is a dream'*. While working say: *'this is a dream'*

Cleaning Energies from the Past .... Chapter 10

- ❖ Write down a list of incidents.
- ❖ Sit in a comfortable posture with your spine straight and hands facing each other; palms relaxed on the knees or at the level of your heart (it might be more comfortable to place them on your knees).
- ❖ Go into your Heart.
- ❖ Initial Breath: Inhale deeply and slowly and, at the same time, bring your hands together, facing each other and without touching. Exhale long and slowly and bring the hands back to the initial position, placed on the knees and facing each other.
- ❖ Take the first incident from the top of your list and remain with it until all the feelings spent in it have been reviewed. Reconstruct the event, piece by piece, starting by recollecting the physical details of the surroundings, then going to the person whom you shared the interaction with and then turning to yourself to examine your feelings.
- ❖ As you remember, a feeling will arise in the event. Inhale deeply and slowly and, at the same time, bring your hands together, facing each other and without touching. The function of this breathing is to restore energy. This is how you pick up the energy that has been left behind.
- ❖ Exhale long and slowly and bring the hands back to the initial position, placed on the knees and facing each

other. By exhaling, the energy that had been left in you by other people who were involved in the event that you are recollecting, will be ejected.

❖ Forgive yourself and the person involved in the incident.

Cleaning the Energy of our Day .... Chapter 11
Turn off the lights, lie down, close your eyes and totally relax.

❖ When you feel either very heavy or so light that you are almost floating, begin looking at your day backwards. It will be as if you are watching a movie; see a form there, but it is not you. You are just a witness, attentive and aware of each activity.

❖ Move back through your day's activities; watch everything as if it is somebody else there, not you. Do not get involved; do not get angry or happy again. Do not get upset or elated.

❖ Start from the moment you got into bed -which is the last activity- and go backwards, step by step, to the first activity in the morning when you first awoke.

Divine Chanting Meditation .... Chapter 13
❖ Move into the Heart.

❖ Place your attention on the first chakra at the base of your body, at your perineum. See a beautiful red color; the mantra word for this chakra is LAM. Chant the mantra LAM gently from your heart, until you feel it spreading throughout your body.

❖ Place your attention on the second chakra behind your navel and see a shining orange-yellow color; the mantra word for this chakra is VAM. Chant the mantra VAM gently from your heart, until you feel it spreading throughout your body.

❖ Place your attention on the third chakra behind the middle of your chest and see a nourishing green color like the grass in springtime; the mantra word for this chakra is YAM. Chant the mantra YAM gently from your heart, until you feel it spreading throughout your body.

❖ Place your attention on the fourth chakra in the middle of your forehead and see a deep dark blue or indigo color, like the night sky on a summer night. This is where the third eye is or the seat of your dreams and visions. The mantra word for this chakra is SHAM; chant the mantra SHAM gently from your heart, until you feel it spreading throughout your body.

❖ Place your attention on the fifth chakra on the top of your head and see a shining gold-white glowing light; this is the crown chakra or the seat of Divinity; the mantra word for this chakra is AUM. Chant the mantra AUM gently from your heart, until you feel it spreading throughout your body.

ABOUT THE AUTHOR

Daniel travels the world, helping people understand their intimate connection to God. He began teaching Zen Meditation in 1981 and he practiced the "spinal breathing" meditation between 1981 and 1992; later he discovered that, in fact, he was practicing Kriya Pranayama of the Kriya Yoga Great Master Babaji.

Since 1996, he has been teaching Meditation Day Workshops and Heart Imagery Workshops worldwide.

After a couple of years spent in meditation in north of Tibet, in 1999, Daniel created *"The School of the Heart"*. Ten years later, in Toronto, he created "The School of Meditation". Daniel is an Ambassador of Peace and Diplomat of Love in the Embassy of Peace.

An international lecturer and Martial Arts Master (Tai Chi Master and Karate Traditional Black Belt 5 DAN in WJKA – World Japan Karate Association), Daniel is dedicated to inspiring the world to move from violence to peace and from anger to love. Throughout his work, workshops and spiritual conferences, Daniel has changed the lives of thousands of people.

Following his practice under the Tibetan Great Lama Masters, Daniel worked with a group of well known Masters from different schools of meditation (Osho, Dalai Lama, Paramahansa Prajnananda, Ana, Di Yu Ming, Sadhguru, Drunvalo Melchizedek, Anastasia) who train their students to be in the Heart. Now, together with his own workshops (**Heart Imagery** and **Kriya Yoga**), Daniel also brings the **Awakening the Illuminated Heart** workshop to the world.

Drunvalo Melchizedek appointed Daniel in the first Council of School of Remembering: Awakening The Illuminated Heart (ATIH)

Teacher's Council. As a Mentor of Drunvalo Melchizedek's School of Remembering, he assisted in training ATIH teachers from all over the world.

With these spiritual seminars, Daniel shares a message of hope and possibility to anyone who wishes to experience a new understanding of life; an understanding which comes from the heart.

Daniel is blessed to work with children, teaching them Tai Chi and Meditation. Daniel had the opportunity to work with Indigo Children from all over the world.

Daniel has an extensive academic background with a B.Sc. degree in Computer Engineering, a B.Econ. (Hons.) Degree, a Diploma in Management and an MBA from the Open University Business School, UK.

Having being interviewed all over the world and constantly invited to write articles in magazines and on-line publications (Spirit of Ma'at, Collective Evolution, Vision, etc.), Daniel is one of the most prominent Masters of Meditations known worldwide, showing the inner power that one can achieve using the Heart's unconditional love.

More information on www.danielmitel.com and
www.heartimagery.org.

In order to help Daniel continue his journey all over the world, please consider contributing a donation by visiting the page on *http://danielmitel.com/donations-and-help/*.
Daniel has made generous donations all over the world to orphanages, homeless shelters, animal shelters and organizations dealing with cleaning the environment.

INDEX